*

The Day of Shelly's Death

*

RENATO ROSALDO

*

THE

DAY OF

SHELLY'S

DEATH

The Poetry and Ethnography of Grief

* * *

DUKE UNIVERSITY PRESS
DURHAM & LONDON
2014

© 2014 Duke University Press
All rights reserved
Printed in the United States of
America on acid-free paper ∞
Designed by Amy Ruth Buchanan
Typeset in Whitman and Lato by
Tseng Information Systems, Inc.

Library of Congress Cataloging-
in-Publication Data
Rosaldo, Renato.
The day of Shelly's death : the poetry and
ethnography of grief / Renato Rosaldo.
pages   cm
Includes bibliographical references.
ISBN 978-0-8223-5649-3 (cloth : alk. paper)
ISBN 978-0-8223-5661-5 (pbk. : alk. paper)
1. Death—Poetry. 2. Ilongot (Philippine people)—
Death. 3. Ethnology in literature. I. Title.
PS3618.O775D39   2014
811'.6—dc23   2013025659

CONTENTS

*

LIST OF POEMS

*

Time Line, 3

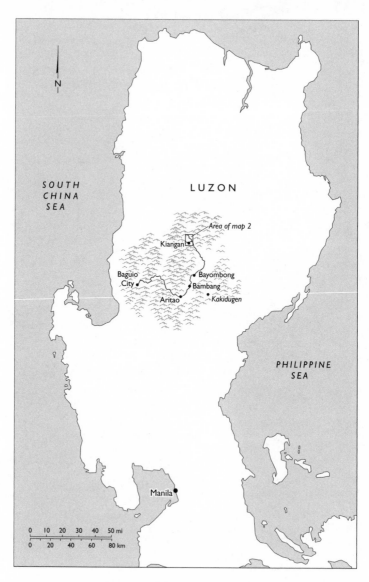

Northern Luzon, Philippines

*

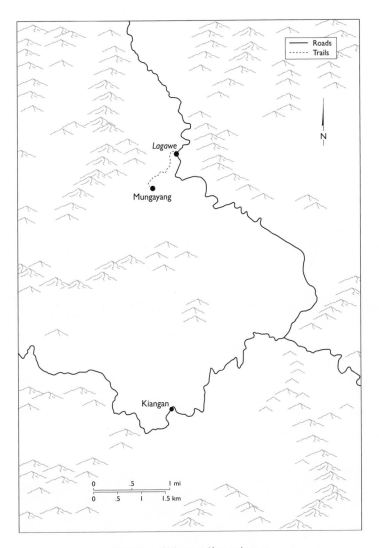

The Area of Kiangan, Ifugao, Luzon

*

ACKNOWLEDGMENTS

*

The following poems have appeared in *Anthropology and Humanism*: "Baket," "How Do I, Renato, Know That Manny Knows," "Silence," "The Tricycle Taxi Driver," and "Tukbaw."

Harold Conklin graciously gave permission to use the three sketches that are figures 19, 20, and 21. Bayninan resident Puggū-won Lupāih drew the sketches; the late Bayninan resident Buwāya Tindōngan wrote the texts on the sketches. I am indebted to Patricia O. Afable who gave permission to use her notes on translations given orally to me by Conklin.

I took all the photographs and Bill Nelson drew the two maps.

I am indebted and grateful to Patricia Spears Jones who first encouraged and then provided fine comments on this collection of poetry. Thank you to Lisa Freedman who commented with care on the poems, and to Sheila Pratt who also gave helpful comments on the poetry manuscript. Two anonymous readers for Duke University Press provided illuminating comments as well. Gisela Fosado, my editor at Duke University Press, served as an incomparable guide.

I am deeply grateful to the bereaved who read these poems and encouraged: Sam Rosaldo, Manuel Rosaldo, Olivia Rosaldo-Pratt, and Andrew Zimbalist. Other family and friends who read and encouraged include: Naima Beckles, Lydia Nettler, Bridget O'Laughlin, and Louise Lamphere. At the beginning of this project Nicole Blackman and Marina García-Vásquez offered encouragement.

Mary Louise Pratt has read, offered insight, and inspired. My gratitude to Mary, my wife, my love, is beyond words.

Shelly Rosaldo's manner of dying still has the power to shock, de-
cades after the event. A well-known feminist and anthropologist,
she fell to her death on October 11, 1981, in a remote region of the
island of Luzon in the Philippines when on a much anticipated
field trip. Hiking from her base to a nearby village and chattering
to her women companions, a slip of the foot sent Shelly hurtling
into a river bed sixty-five feet below. It is not easy to imagine those
final seconds when the last flash of thought was about to be extin-
guished. For most of us in these secular times there is no language
momentous enough to describe or account for "accidental death";
the word "accident" derives from *Ad cadere*, that is, to fall and the
fall can no longer be attributed to God or to the Fates.

With her husband and fellow anthropologist, Renato Rosaldo,
and her two sons, Sam age five and Manny a mere fourteen months,
she had arrived in the village of Mungayang, which was inhabited
by a tightly knit group of Ifugao speakers. The American scholars
were undaunted by the challenge of doing research and looking
after their children among people whose language they did not yet
speak and in the militarized country presided over by Ferdinand
Marcos. Shelly and Renato were, after all, seasoned anthropologists
and were used to combining fieldwork with family life. Theirs was
an equal partnership and on the first day, they had tossed a coin
to see who would stay behind with the children and who would go
to a nearby village where they hoped to carry out their research.
Shelly had won and, in retrospect, had lost. It was as if an archaic
design had infiltrated modernity. It was as if the gods, the eternal
spoilers, were out for punishment. In one of Renato's poems, he
describes himself as flowing "past the gate/ as if through a funnel/
to the other side."

Loss cannot be easily overcome. I do not believe that we can, in any simple way, put mourning behind us. There is a long sequel of rage and sadness after an untimely death. Renato Rosaldo's poems, written over many years, expose the hollowness of "coming to terms" or "getting over it." It is poetry not ethnography that has enabled him to grasp "how deep rage could grow out of grief," a poetry that seeks an understanding of loss and that speaks of it in something other than the individual voice. Renato uses a metaphor from photography, "depth of field," to express what he strives for in this mourning poetry in which his grief does not occur in isolation but ripples outward and is witnessed. It is a loss that affected in various degrees villagers and all those fortuitously caught up in the aftermath of disaster. His poetry, as he himself puts it, is "informed by ethnographic sensibility." Comparing it to the thick description of his discipline, he describes it as a poetry that "points to real things in the world." Those real things encompass the numbing reality of loss that is both solitary and shared, solitary as he watches a fly crawl over Shelly's face and recognizes the finality of death, and shared when he must face the difficulty of looking after his children, finding transport, reporting the death to the authorities, and accompanying the corpse through military checkpoints toward Manila. Great grief must cope with the mundane and often bureaucratic aftermath.

Rosaldo's "anthropoetry" reaches beyond the narrative of personal loss and gives voice to a chorus of villagers, officials, priests, nuns, and the children; and it is through their oblique view that the singular becomes plural, that the personal loss does not occur in isolation but within a social network reimagined by the poet so that the villagers of Mungayang whom they had scarcely got to know and the people Renato meets on the arduous journey back to Manila become the chorus and the places that he and Shelly had traveled together, stages in the bureaucracy of death. Not for nothing did the ancients envisage death as a journey.

The photographs that accompany the poems are the melancholy records of that now-distant past, a counterpoint to poems that speak in a perpetual present.

—Jean Franco

PART I

*

Shelly and I are on leave from Stanford where we teach cultural anthropology.

We're on a Fulbright to teach this school year (1981–82) at the University of the Philippines College in Baguio City, which is high and cool compared with Manila.

Friday, August 7, 1981, we arrive in Manila with our sons Sam and Manny. Sam is four and Manny turned one on July 28.

After a week in Manila, we reach Baguio City, Friday, August 14, where we plan to stay for the school year, until June of 1982.

This fall semester we'll meet with faculty to plan courses and research projects.

During the spring semester we'll teach Philippine Ethnography, Methods, and Development.

In the summer we plan field research in an Ifugao village yet to be selected.

Friday, September 4, at 7 a.m. we fly east by small plane from Baguio to Kakidugen in Ifugao country.

That noon we eat at Lakay's house by the airstrip and that night we sleep at the house of Tepeg and Midalya's married son.

Saturday, September 5, we sleep at Tukbaw and Wagat's house.

Sunday, September 6, we sleep at Tepeg and Midalya's house.

Monday, September 7, we sleep at Lakay's house by the airstrip.

Tuesday, September 8, the Piper Cub arrives for us at 8:30 a.m. and we fly to Aritao. From there we travel by bus, jeepney, and Ford Fiera to Kiangan in Ifugao country.

Friday, September 11, we travel by bus from Kiangan to Baguio where we stay for about a month.

Thursday, October 8, we travel by bus from Baguio to Kiangan.

Friday, October 9, we meet with Father Joe and Conchita Cumaldi to plan the next day's trip to Mungayang.

Saturday, October 10, we take a jeepney from Kiangan to Lagawe, then walk down a steep hill to Mungayang.

Sunday, October 11, Shelly walks toward another village with Conchita Cumaldi and her cousin. On the trail, Shelly falls to her death.

Conchita takes me to where Shelly fell, then we return to Mungayang.

That afternoon we walk up the steep hill to Lagawe.

That night I accompany Shelly's body to a funeral parlor in the Magat Valley town of Bayombong. Later that night I return to the convent where Sam and Manny are sleeping.

Monday, October 12, Father Joe drives me, Sam, and Manny from the convent to Baguio City.

OCTOBER 11, 1981

SILENCE

Subtract from the village hum
        a pestle pounding grains of rice
        the swoosh of a winnowing tray
        rice bubbling on the fire
        chickens clucking in the yard
        soft voices of women at work.

Bird songs stop.
Conchita Cumaldi arrives.
Don't panic, she says.

EDGES OF TRANQUILITY

Water   flows   on the edges
of rice terraces   labor   of centuries
rim   of trough   crumbles.

Boys   howl   in moonlight
words   I cannot   understand
sounds   I cannot   help but fear.

Shelly's   touch   calms
as we   plan   days on beach
speak   our love   and sleep.

Morning   in a wooden hut   rice boils
our baby   Manny   whimpers
a burp   then he   vomits.

Manny sighs   I rub   his back
Sam rests   his head   on my lap
a flock of songbirds   now   silent.

The same. The very spot where I fell. I told Shelly and Renato seven years ago when we met at the Beyer Lodge in Banawe, I told them.

At the time I used crutches, my leg broken in a fall on the trail near Mungayang, rough patch, the rim of an irrigation trough.

The exact spot where Shelly fell today, pulled to her death, hill to one side, sheer drop to the other. I fell toward the hill, fighting tentacles wrapped round my ankles and wrists.

Heathen spirits cackled, mocking my crucifix. These spirits follow whims, not my will. Wish I could trade with Shelly. The two boys need their mother.

I tell the health officer Shelly probably died between noon and
  one.

Time of injury
> *October 11, 1981*
> *12:30 P.M.*

I say she died in Mungayang.

Place of death
> *Barrio Mungayang   Town of Kiangan   Ifugao province.*

I tell him she fell from a cliff into the river. After he writes, I
  remind him of the river.

How injury occurred
> *She fell into the precipice*
> *down the river.*

The health officer walks over to Shelly's body, comes back, and
  writes.

The disease or conditions directly leading to death
> *Contused   lacerated   wounds multiple   head and face*
> *due to accidental fall from the precipice.*

I say nothing more.

I hereby certify that the foregoing particulars are correct
> *Arsenio M. Lopez, M.D., C.P.H.*
> *Provincial Health Office*

I WAS WALKING

My steps measured
the trail visible ahead

until I flowed past the gate
as if through a funnel
to the other side

my vision gone
the gate lost behind
all changed utterly

as if my right arm gone
what most sustained me
gone.

KAKIDUGEN, EARLY SEPTEMBER 1981

Shelly, our two sons, and I arrived at Lakay's home in the Ilongot settlement of Kakidugen where we did field research for three years (1967–1969 and 1974). People gathered and killed a chicken for our welcome meal.

The meal also celebrated our sons, almost five and fourteen months. Our older son Sam was pained that he spoke no Ilongot. After we ate, he dropped to the rattan floor of the house and began writhing. At first our hosts were upset, but when he smiled and went back to twisting on the floor they shrieked with delight. They understood he was imitating the chicken's last moments.

After our visit, we fly to Aritao and travel overland, with a stop in Kiangan, to Baguio.

Kakidugen, landscape, pollarded trees foreground

*

Kakidugen, landscape

*

A man pollarding a tree

*

Houses

*

Rice granaries

*

Taru

*

TARU

I never figure in men's talk.
Tukbaw says in a dispute I'm simple, a mumbler.

Nato and Seli, our names for Renato and Shelly, listen
to my half-brother Tukbaw, neglect me, never ask for my stories,
but today Nato asks me the name of a plant.

I know plants, their names, their uses, where and how they grow.
My mother taught me the ways of plants.
Nato had not asked, must have thought they had no names.

Oozing sores cover my body, no woman wants me.
No bachelor among us lives alone, my cousins take me in.

Years of coughing blood have made me gaunt.
Death has come close and three times I've recuperated.

Wagat

*

I'm married to Tukbaw, no children. He had none with Biya.
I'm a sour rattan fruit, forehead furrowed, tongue sharp.
What a couple we were! Tukbaw thin of waist, eloquent,

a man of influence. I quick of step, hard-working.
Now I harp that Tukbaw's a long-mouthed fish,
always talking, never working around the house.

He orates through the night,
his oblique, flowery speech soothes bruised feelings,
tires him. He does for others what he doesn't do for me.

He settles all grudges but mine.
Tukbaw proudly tells Nato the story of his life,
nothing in it for me.

Our adopted Ifugao daughter does chores, speaks our language.
May she bring joy in my old age.

Tukbaw

*

As I age pain shoots from my back to my legs.
When the pain intensifies, Nato takes me to the hospital in
    Bambang.

Lowlanders there speak Ilocano. I pretend not to understand and
    overhear
their plot to kill me in my sleep simply because I am an Ilongot.

In Kakidugen people listen as I orate. I'm the son of Baket,
married to Wagat who calls me a long-mouthed fish.

Does she think oratory nothing but speaking?
I listen for what's hidden, call out the hearts of others

then sit by the hearth like a rooster stroking its coxcomb
as I weave many hearts into one.

The doctors advise Nato to stay in the hotel, but he sleeps in the
    hospital,
nods when in Kakidugen I say that, like a brother, he didn't
    abandon me.

Lakay

*

LAKAY

I'm the oldest man in Kakidugen,
father of Insan, Tepeg, and Wagat.
When I talk about the past, Insan interrupts,
Don't garble your story.

I weep for the men I knew from boyhood, now gone.
Young men think me an old fool who cries for no reason.

Nato asks for my stories, lets me finish each one.
I tell how the Butags beheaded my uncle
but my nephews beg me not to finish.
This story calls them to avenge their grandfather.

I weep for the men I knew from boyhood, now gone.
Young men think me an old fool who cries for no reason.

On their first visit Nato and Seli lived
in our house, ate our food, learned
our language. They're clumsy
can't peel sugar cane, stumble on the trail.

I weep for the men I knew from boyhood, now gone.
Young men think me an old fool who cries for no reason.

Even if I can't tie a knot or clear the forest
as I once did, even if I only lead the dogs,
never wait in ambush for running deer or wild pig,
even if I forget a name or part of the story,
I am the source.

I weep for the men I knew from boyhood, now gone.
Young men think me an old fool who cries for no reason.

Insan

*

INSAN

In the hunt I shoot fast, no wild pig escapes me.
My name is Insan, son of Lakay. My wife is Duman.
I have no patience with fancy speech.
I'm outgoing, my words direct, not like a woman.

Nato asks me when he needs to know
why feuds flared or about the movements
of settlements, even if I can't recall
who said what or the sequence of events,
I know the politics.

I cannot bear the pain of my father's failing.
He forgets when his nephews hear
of their grandfather's beheading
their desire for vengeance grows severe.

Duman

*

I AM DUMAN

I'm married to Insan.
I tell him the ways of other men,
show him how to be savvy in politics.

Nato sees me at work without a blouse
so I have to tell my story.

One of my breasts is small, smashed
long ago in a sugar cane press — pain
worse than front teeth filed to my gums.

I teach Seli how to wrap our skirts
tie them with brass belt, push
the cloth between her legs as she sits.

Seli and I share betel nut as we talk of others.
Gossip and laughter seal our friendship.

I talk about Lana. Her house out of rice.
She listens for the pounding of rice at our house,
drops by at mealtime.

Seli had noticed.

Baket

*

BAKET

I was a girl when Lakay was born,
his oldest daughter Wagat married my son Tukbaw
his son Tepeg married my daughter Midalya.

My grandchildren seek my wisdom,
trust me to guard their secrets,
their passions, and their wounds.

They say I know nothing,
but I once said what they now say.

I tell Nato the few stories of adultery in Kakidugen.
It's more common, he says, in his land.
Oh no, I say, it spread from Kakidugen.

Now I tend a small garden, no rice,
mustard greens and sweet potatoes to feed
the sow I've raised since I held her in one hand.

My fame reaches from Tamsi to Sigem. My pet
fed a hot meal every day. Too fat to walk, too heavy to carry.
How, my grandchildren ask, will I take her to market in Kasibu?

I say I'll have three young men guide my pig,
a slow pace, six nights in the forest.

Tepeg

Tepeg and Seli (Shelly)

*

TEPEG

says he's less handsome than
his brother Insan. Husband to Midalya.

He mocks men less shy, men of influence
repeats news of the day, spoken earlier

as humdrum daily chatter now replayed
as ragged mimicry. In the high tones of oratory

he tells low stories — Tukbaw's dog injured
its paw, Wagat has taken to bed with a cold.

He and Shelly transcribe varieties of speech
he claims not to know, though he deciphers

their riddle-like contours and repeats
rapid exchanges verbatim, defining each word

in several ways, explaining the politics
of local disputes, such as Kenga's demand

for a carabao in exchange for his sister's hand
in marriage. It's exorbitant and will be fought

with elegant, oblique phrases. He claims
his tongue stumbles, but he's a nimble

word dancer who in his own home
sings, orates, chants hunting spells.

You, spirit who walks by the river,
come join my steaming here!

Here I steam magic on my hand
by the hearthstone.

Midalya and family

Midalya

*

MIDALYA

She says she has nothing to say, thin, haggard,
Tukbaw her brother, her husband Tepeg
a man heavier than most.

Shelly and I, Renato, live in their home for a year.

I say,
We're the same as you.
  We eat your food
    sleep on your floor.

Midalya says
I keep your house
  cook your food.
    I am your maid.

Midalya's words have weight
spoken as matter of fact.
I cannot but accept their truth.

On our visit of 1981 Midalya huddles
Shelly and me in a dark corner by the hearth.
She weeps, saying farewell, urging
us to be careful, her premonition insisting
what she divines and I as yet do not know.

Shelly

Renato

*

BAGUIO,
LATE AUGUST TO EARLY OCTOBER, 1981

In Baguio we looked into hiring a maid to give us time to teach and do our research. The first person we tried spoke neither English nor Tagalog. We couldn't communicate and finally had to fire her. She left in tears. We did not want to repeat that experience.

The next woman we hired immediately asked to borrow my type-writer. I needed it to write my field journal and a review of Hal Conklin's *Ethnographic Atlas of Ifugao*, but I lent it to her because I didn't want to give offence. She worked all day and into the night on a letter to her former employer. With only a fourth grade education, writing a letter of even a few pages was an arduous task for her. I was miffed.

On Sunday, September 20, 1981, we celebrated Sam's fifth birthday with cake, ice cream, streamers, balloons, and nearby friends. Unfortu-nately, that day some people couldn't come because of pelting rain and terrible wind—a typhoon was passing through town and drivers feared falling trees.

Although we've been in the Philippines three weeks now (and
Baguio two), have an apartment (with guest space, should
you visit), a "helper" (Philippine English for "maid"), Sam in
kindergarten, and us involved in numerous promises to give
lectures here, advice there. . . . I have the feeling that I can't write
a letter because in some ways "nothing has happened."

Which means not that nothing has happened, but that the
shift in pace from the last days in Palo Alto has been so radical
that my overwhelming feeling (complemented, of course, by
the amount of time it takes indirect and rather status conscious
Filipinos to say anything in meetings; then again, by the tentative,
awkward, strained partial communications with our non-English
speaking "helper"; then again by the fact that it's fun to lounge on
the streets and in markets, making the quest for bananas a bit of
"meaning" all by itself) is one of ease.

"Home" does seem impossibly distant. Sam talks more about it
than either of us.

One evening in Baguio
we're invited to a family dinner
with a woman,

a commander in the New People's Army,
and her brother,
a captain in the military under Marcos.

Their mother seats us
in the precarious space between.
What will brother and sister say?

Over dinner they speak only about
what Imelda, the First Lady,
will wear at Sadat's funeral.

They fight
over her look, Miami Vice
versus Princess Di,

over whether her dress
will be designed by Christian Dior
or Ralph Lauren,

but by dessert they agree,
not folkloric,
not a mestiza gown.

Nena, our Ifugao language teacher and new friend, said she would come with us to Kiangan, but the night before our departure she said she could not travel because her nephew of four had just fallen from a stone wall. I forget Nena's exact words, but remember shuddering as I pictured a boy falling, upside-down, arms flailing.

We took a bus to the Ifugao town of Kiangan at the end of the first week of October. An elderly man, the uncle of our host-to-be in Kiangan, happened to be on the bus. When we got off to stretch in Bambang, Sam worried that we might be left behind, but we assured him that buses never do that. As the bus pulled out of town, Sam noticed that the old man was not on board. We told the driver and he immediately returned to town. Several passengers who spoke English said, "We abandoned our grandfather and only your little boy noticed."

At St. Joseph's church in Kiangan, Sister Doris tells us to meet Father Joe who, like her, has been in Kiangan many years. He's out in the villages so we can't meet him today. She expresses great concern for our safety, then says a suitable fieldwork site might be Mungayang where a woman named Conchita Cumaldi is the catechist. Conchita can be trusted.

Manny must perch
on the big chair
feet dangling,

can't crawl on floor
covered with gray dust,
bags of cement in piles.

Our host was told
the job would be finished,
haggles with us over the price

of the upstairs room,
a bed with mosquito net.
Shelly and I notice

but say nothing.
Instead we put Sam
and Manny in the bed

and lie down to sleep
beside our sons on a mat
on the floor.

Downstairs, Jun's brother
laughs with Sam, gives him
the name of a leader, Kemayong.

Jun's brother asks for a scotch,
then a Constabulary lieutenant
and an Ilocano store owner arrive.

They agree Sadat was a good man,
anti-Communist.
The store owner rails

that local priests favor the NPA,
that blacks in Philadelphia lowered
the value of his cousins' homes.

Knowingly, they offend,
display their power, drink,
and play poker until dawn.

Outside Jun's house
Ifugao children gather
to meet Sam.

Sam collects himself
lips tight
eyes gray

and steps out
gives his name
Kemayong.

Kemayong the children repeat
and they smile.
He curls his fingers

round his eyes
face of an owl.
Sam skips

down the trail
with the children.
Returns in tears.

NO SWIMMER

The river turns brown,
swells, churns, rises, dives, slants.

No raft rides its surface
no swimmer dares its current.

On high ground men and women teeter
as if on a precipice.

Persistent rumors,
Soldiers at checkpoints torture suspects
bodies   mutilated   bullet riddled.

CONCHITA CAN BE TRUSTED

In a time of only two sides,
the for and the against,

both sides say,
Conchita can be trusted.

She navigates
the churning middle.

We ask her to be our guide.
Conchita musters,
I shall be the one.

CONCHITA CUMALDI

In Mungayang I'm catechist
and barrio captain.

Father Joe asks
me to be the guide
for Renato and Shelly.

I have no choice
but to say,
I shall be the one.

I walk with integrity,
live by my word.

MUNGAYANG, OCTOBER 10, 1981

With Conchita, we rode a jeepney from Kiangan to Lagawe, then walked down a steep hill and reached the village of Mungayang in the afternoon. Sam walked the whole way. He delighted the kids there by saying his name was Kemayong and by playing with them. Shelly was so happy she promised to buy him a Leggo set and a ten-flavor ice cream sundae when we returned to Baguio.

Mungayang lies on a small shelf of flat land with a river nearby. Unlike Kakidugen, it's a compact village, not scattered houses. Rice grows in irrigated pond fields rather than in rain-fed gardens. The Ilongot and Ifugao languages are so different we can understand nothing.

We like Mungayang. It seems a good place to spend two or three months doing fieldwork after the end of the school year. And it's near the clinic in Lagawe should Sam or Manny need a doctor.

NEW SHOES

In Mungayang the day is hot,
the night cool, the moon full.
Our tired sons sleep.

The screams of Ifugao teen-age boys
make me soothe Renato.
He and I talk of shoes he bought

for Sam and me, soles with furrowed tread,
a gift to keep us safe.
We speak of Nana Dot's visit soon this fall

to where we are, our likely fieldwork site.
We joke that Manny need not learn to talk,
his babble artfully communicates.

We glow in this good beginning
and vow romance on evening dinner dates,
a week at sandy beach. We whisper low,

touch fingertips and caress
in long embrace, then sleep the night.

TURBULENCE

Teen-age boys howl.
Do they crave our heads?
We're tempting targets, two strangers.

I can't understand their screams.
Stones crack against a wall.
I wonder if they howl lust.

Conchita yells at the boys,
walks over, talks to them, tells Shelly
and me it's not about us.

MUNGAYANG, OCTOBER 11, 1981

SHOES ON MY HEAD

It's Sunday, October 11, 1981,
the day of Shelly's death.

Last night she and I talked,
touched fingertips.

This morning Shelly put her nose
in Manny's tummy, his delight flowed in giggles.

I placed Manny's shoes on my head,
we rolled on the floor in laughter.

Then Shelly walked with Conchita.
I napped with our two sons.

The morning after the full moon
our baby burps and clear liquid splats
into the wall.
        Shelly and Conchita hike
toward a village upstream. I nap
with our sons, one and five years old.
A flock of songbirds
abruptly silent.
        Minutes later, Conchita
steps into the hut and rasps, *She fell
into the river.* I run, reach Shelly's body, drop
to her side. A fly buzzes in, then out of her mouth.

Back on the trail, Shelly's voice, not the wind, her voice
echoes from death. I rush
to our sons.
        Conchita's cousin lifts Manny on her back,
then crumples into sobs.

I put Sam on my shoulders, tell him his mom is dead.
He wants to know when he will get a new one.

A MOUSE

It scurries
across smooth brown planks

seeks human droppings
cooked grains of rice
bits of sweet potato.

Conchita shouts the news.
Mungayang falls silent.

Mice give birth
die.

Birth
looking for droppings
death.

HOW DO I, RENATO, KNOW THAT MANNY KNOWS?

That morning in Mungayang,
Manny shoots vomit in a straight line across the room.

We toss a coin. Tails. I stay. Shelly walks with Conchita.
Day one of our ethnographic survey.

Manny babbles, saying gibble gibble,
happily cooing. Then he abruptly screeches
a piercing sound that ricochets

through the dark wooden hut
penetrating like a mouse that scurries
across smooth brown planks.

Conchita steps in the hut, says, *Don't panic*,
takes me to the place where Shelly stumbled
from a precipice to the swollen, brown river.

When I return and hug Manny, my trembling
touch fails to reassure.
Bags packed quickly. Conchita's cousin lifts Manny
onto her back. He sobs, low and long. She collapses.
I put Sam on my shoulders,
walk the steep hill to Lagawe.

The next day a priest drives Manny, Sam, and me
down to the Magat Valley   hot   hotter

then up a winding mountain road   cooling   cooler.
Manny grows giddy, giggling insistently.

In Baguio City I carry him into our apartment.
He searches   swivels   nobody here.

He bellows and shatters
the enormous thick silence.

CONCHITA'S COUSIN

My cousin needs
a trusted companion on the trail.

She asks me to walk
with her and the blond American woman.

The American walks, head high,
talking and talking, even a few Ifugao words.

She talks to Conchita, ahead of her.
A few paces back, I walk in silence.

The American woman stumbles
reaches toward me.
I scream, Conchita turns.

I lunge to grab her.

Her arms stretch toward me
but she drops slowly
says not a word.

**   **

We rush toward the village of Mungayang,
shout for the men

to wait at the riverbend where we know
the body will wash ashore.

**   **   **

In the afternoon, we gather to walk
uphill to the town of Lagawe.

I put the American baby in his yellow backpack,
lift him on my back.

He screams, I collapse.

YELLOW BACKPACK

Holes for Manny's legs
interrupt
bright yellow nylon.
Padded shoulder straps
and curved aluminum bars
on either side spread
his weight as he places
his arms on the shoulders
of a stranger.

BE CAREFUL

Don't panic,
I say.
Must tell Renato
little by little,
not shock
the soul
out of his body.

Is she alive?
Conchita, please tell me, Renato says.
I say she fell.
How far? he asks.

I say I'll show him the place,
ask him to wear shoes,
but he rushes out in flip-flops.

Again he asks,
How far did she fall?
He looks down the cliff,
a drop of over sixty feet
swollen river below.

I slow the pace, tell him,
Be careful.
We reach the spot
and I say Shelly and I
were talking,
her voice full of life,
a few words in Ifugao.

Somber, silent, ashen—he knows.
Walking back, I call the men,
finally a reply.
Is she alive? he asks
and runs down the hill.

Shelly said she was wearing
reliable shoes.

KEY:

A   hiŋŋul: the inner bend of a mountain

B   pūduŋ hinan potoq di nagahāna: arrow grass marker at the place where Shelly fell

C   timmiqāyuŋ: a rough declivity with nothing to hold onto

D   qoŋal qan batuh nan banoŋ di qālaq: a boulder beneath the wall of the irrigation channel

E   nahaqqad qan doplah: the steepness of the rock cliff

NOTES:

(B)   Pūduŋ hinan potoq di nagahāna: pūduŋ, a Miscanthus stem with top leaves tied in a knot, stuck into the ground, is used as a marker at the specific place [hinan potoq] where Shelly fell [di nagahāna]. For pūduŋ, see Leonard E. Newell, *Batad Ifugao Dictionary with Ethnographic Notes*. Manila: Linguistic Society of the Philippines, 1993.

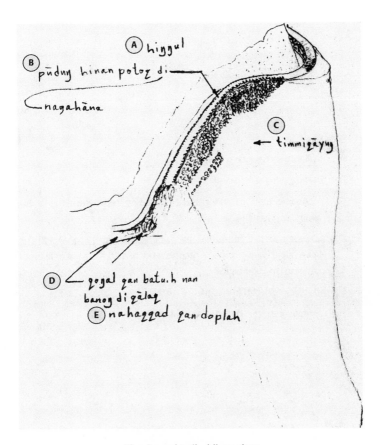

The rim and trail, oblique view

*

KEY:

A   qālaq: an irrigation channel

B   qallup: a two-sided wall

C   nahaqpāan: a buttress terrace, a protruding step made in the stone wall

D   duwampūlu nin metloh di tinagēna mihīpun hinan qālaq ta naŋā-muŋ hinan waŋwaŋ: it is perhaps twenty meters from the irrigation ditch to the river below

E   dopla: a rock cliff (misspelling for doplah)

F   waŋwaŋ: a river (Ifugaos don't name rivers)

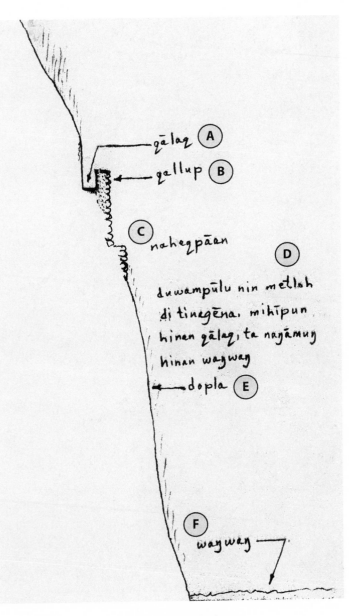

The rim and trail, side view

*

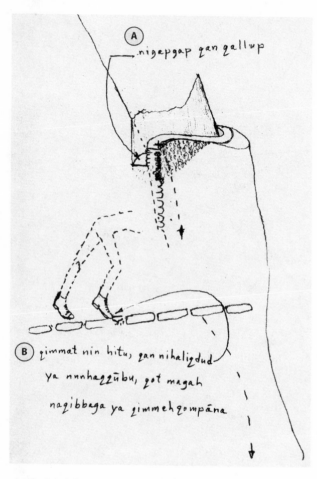

Shelly's fall, cross-section, and oblique view of rim and trail

*

KEY:

A   nigapgap qan qallup: a cross-section of the wall

B   qimmat nin hitu, qan nihaliqdud ya nunhaqqūbu, qot
magah naqibbaga ya qimmehqompāna: perhaps this is
how she fell, perhaps she stumbled on a notch in the top
of the wall and immediately fell down below

A RIM

An Ifugao
rice terrace
whose rim
crumbles at
one spot
a slender
ledge where
trough carries
water and
rim disintegrates
under feet
of walkers.

THE IFUGAO MEN

They heed Conchita's call,
run to the river bank,

squat, look upstream,
talk in low tones, intercept

the American woman's body
washing toward shore,

carry it to land, form a circle,
stand silent. Conchita arrives

with a pale, trembling man.
He places his lips on the body's lips,

rocks back. A fly buzzes
in then out of the body's mouth.

THE FLY

I stare at the fly.
One back leg rubs
the other.

Sky and earth heave,
press together.

Pressure
on my lungs,
tidal welling

overwhelms
my exhalation.

SHELLY'S BODY WASHED

We stop in Mungayang.
At last soft tears flow, cry soft easy tears
until Conchita asks

if I want
Shelly's body washed.
To dress her

I choose
brown pants,
pale green shirt.

I cannot leave
Shelly's nightgown,
her *Middlemarch*,

then tell Sam and Manny
we'll soon leave,
Mom will catch up.

I pack a pacifier
diapers   a toy truck   pajamas
Tintin in America.

THE SOLDIER

My assignment, municipal center,
Kiangan, not yet Christian,

grandparents headhunters.
Tourists visit rice terraces, infested,

guerrilla cadres, New People's Army.
To them my ears cut off
as much a trophy as my ArmaLite.

My captain's orders:
post-haste to Mungayang,
American woman dead, investigate
possible homicide. Chief suspect
her husband. Report by afternoon.
No time, don't change
from jungle camoflauge.

Here's the man I was sent to find.
I order him to stop,
my ArmaLite at the ready,
Was there foul play? I ask.
No, he says, *it was an accident.*

He's pale, trembling, trudging,
with him two sons, a little boy and a baby.
In him I see
the same
ashen face
knotted shoulders
automaton walk
my father had
the day my mother died.
The same.

I tell the pale, trembling man
investigation's over.
No reason to linger.

I walk the hill double-time,
reach barracks by early afternoon.

LAGAWE, OCTOBER 11, 1981

Dad says Mom's coming,
gives me a shoulder ride,
once I'm up, says she died.

A low branch. I duck.
Dad's back wet,
muscles like rock.

At least I'm not riding
in yellow backpack,
like a baby.

Dad pants
up a steep hill
to the place

where an orange
and red tricycle taxi
is waiting.

THE TRICYCLE TAXI DRIVER

Please accept my gift, I say.

In Lagawe I own the only
tricyle taxi, orange, yellow, red,
fresh paint, curving lines.

After noon the soldiers arrive breathless,
say an American woman fell
from the precipice near Mungayang.

At dusk they arrive, Ifugaos, a few men,
two women, one carries the baby
of the American woman in a yellow backpack.

I shall be the one.

In a rattan hammock tied to a pole
Ifugao men bring the woman's body.
The American man shoulders

his five-year-old son,
his walk heavy, shirt soaked,
face streaked with dirt,

his tears behind red eyes,
then he mumbles,
Taxi, and steps toward me.

He places his two sons on the seats,
then sits between them, offers to pay.
I've come here to give him a ride.

Please accept my gift, I say.

A THIN SMILE

Here's the American whose wife died today.
I give my name, Alfredo Evangelista,
tell how my wife's
miscarriage opened
me to his agony.

My loss, the funeral for little Emma,
not the same as a love of fifteen years,
two boys, no mother,
but it's all I can muster.

My paltry loss shames me.
In tears I say, *Condolences.*

With a thin smile, the American stands silent,
moved, perhaps, beyond words.

At the clinic in Lagawe strangers form a crowd and stare at me. One man with a cheery smile asks, *How did it happen?* The room fades to very white.

The Ifugao men place Shelly's body on a stone slab in the morgue. There they will stand vigil through the night. Conchita says she's going for Father Joe. I'm left without a rudder.

A woman from the pharmacy asks for the American. I nod. She hands me diapers, sodas, snacks, and mosquito nets. I feed Sam and Manny in a back room, lie them down to sleep.

A nurse pulls the gray sheet from Shelly's face. Blood and bruises. The doctor tells me to take the body to Solano to be embalmed. It is up to me, she says. I say, no. No, I will not leave my sons alone here.

The Mayor of Lagawe shouts, *How could you allow your wife to walk the trail alone? Why don't you embalm the body here in Lagawe?*

Father George says, *Never mind the Mayor, he's drunk,* then drives me and the boys to the convent in a VW bug.

NIGHT, OCTOBER 11, 1981

I can't reconstruct where we slept the night of Shelly's death. Father George took us in a vw bug to a convent, but it was pitch black and raining hard. I sat in the back seat caring for Sam and Manny, not paying attention to where we were going.

STATIC

I drive the American
and his sons to the convent,
take him to a small room, low ceiling,
dim light. Crackles from a short-wave radio

make him shudder. I ask if he wants
to talk with Jules in Baguio, my classmate,
fellow Belgian, once a priest, now
an anthropologist, the American's friend.
He nods yes.

Renato says, *Shelly fell to her death, an accident. Over.*

Jules says, *I know. How are you? And the boys? Over.*

Renato says, *Father Joe will drive us to Baguio tomorrow. See you
    soon. Over and out.*

How could the American know
the reach of shock
and sympathy in this land
where grief lives in public?

He's pale, shaking,
like a boxer he keeps
his guard up, feet heavy.

HOMILIES

Father George says

In one week your sons will feel the loss.

In two weeks you will feel the loss.

Allow women to nurture your sons or they'll hate the opposite sex.

Spend a week in solitude, know your essential aloneness.

Observe one year of mourning. Otherwise people will talk.

SAM AT THE CONVENT

An old nun brings
paper, pencils, crayons.

I scribble, then draw
a beautiful witch,
red lips, black dress, white coat.

The witch flies in the window,
dances out the door with Dad,
out the door they dance.

out the door they leave,
they leave, leaving
me and Manny.

JUN DAIT

I'm a big man here in Kiangan,
my body has heft.
That Ford Fiera is mine.

I met Renato at Skyland Travel in Baguio,
invited the family to stay in my home,
makes me look good.

Grandpa says I must run for office.
My brother will be forced from politics,
he's a drunk who bullies and batters.

I support Marcos, must protect
my investments, mining, real estate,
an Ifugao folkart store in Manila.

That damned American
will never thank me enough.
I've opened my house to him.

Now I accompany him, Kiangan
to Bayombong and back, late at night
to avoid traffic at checkpoints

where I tell the soldiers
why there is
a corpse in our car.

ONE NIGHT AND THE NEXT

Conchita calls for quiet,
denies the teen-age boys' screams
are about us, but she won't translate.

Shelly calm, I apprehensive.
That night, I sleep in her arms.

Next night, heavy rain,
gravel roads, abrupt turns,
military checkpoints, precarious drops.

A journey in the dark of night.
Shelly's body in a wooden casket.

MIDNIGHT DRIVER

I'm Jun's driver.
The pale, trembling man
offers heartfelt thanks,

his name Renato, but nobody knows
my name, the back of a head behind the wheel.

Late night round trip — Kiangan to Bayombong —
carrying a dead body and the husband who shudders
each time a checkpoint soldier requests

the death certificate. *This is not
just a piece of paper* he says

then drifts into silence
through clouded black on narrow road,
hair-pin turns, steep drops.

My focus shrouds me
passengers trust my velocity
will be measured, my senses sure.

In my darkest hour of need
let there be a no-name driver to transport me.

THE CLIFF

I stretch
from precipice
to river
the American
woman fell
along my
rocky spine
contusions on
her face
no autopsy
no way
to check
for water
in lungs
to know
if rocks
or river
the cause
of death
but I
am blamed
though I
never wanted
this day
of lamentation.

Tonight Renato must accompany the corpse to Funeraria Gambito in Bayombong. In our care he leaves his sons. The baby, long blond curls, darling blue eyes.

The two boys sit together, say nothing, big brother protects baby. I touch the boy's shoulder, he shoves my hand, looks up, asks my name. *Sister Doris.*

I say his dad has gone to care for his mom's body. The boy says, *I know, Dad told me.*

I say his mom has gone to a better place. He crosses his arms, sits straight, lips pinched. I tell him his mom will visit in a dream.

When I return from Funeraria Gambito I find
the door to Sam and Manny's room locked.
The catechist who took the key
won't return until dawn.
I lie down in my room.
At 3:18 a.m. the air is cold.
In the first light of dawn
I go to their room
lie on the mat by the door
which is finally opened.
Sam speaks from a circle of calm
I dreamt Mom
became a star to protect me.

THE ROAD, OCTOBER 12, 1981

COLORED MARSHMALLOWS

In Bayombong Father Joe arranges
for Shelly's body to be transported to Manila.
We wait in a windowless room.

Sam lies listless on my lap,
asks for stories, one after another.

I buy colored marshmallows
for Manny who glistens red
and screams and screams.

FATHER JOE

I'm Bontoc, raised
to grow rice, not to serve
as a Catholic priest.
I know tribal wisdom,
the cruelty of lowlanders.
I walk the villages weeks on end,
my skin purple with trekking.
I insist on social justice.
Its absence corrodes.

I know Renato and Shelly.
They're progressive.
Faith in the people
makes critical anthropology
like my liberation theology.
I ache with Shelly's death,
barely knew her,
but the loss is bitter.

I drive Renato and his sons
the eight hours to Baguio City.
When we stop for lunch in Aritao
I tell people there
Renato's wife died yesterday.
An old man touches
his chest, gasps in English, *Condolences.*
A silly Ilocana says sexy man
and asks me if the American wants
a *yaya* to care for his sons.

Renato asks what there is to say.
No words, I say, no words.

BAGUIO, OCTOBER 12, 1981

In Baguio I phone Jules. He comes to our apartment with his wife and two friends. Jules gives me a glass of scotch, sits by me, and holds my hand as I speak with Shelly's mom and my parents.

NANA DOT

Renato called today from the Philippines,
said Shelly died, fell from a cliff, an accident.
My only daughter left two sons,

Sam and Manny.
Stupid, stupid, stupid, stupid.
How could she leave so much behind?

I get such nachas from introducing
the whole mishpocha table to table
at the Lake Success swimming pool.

Must talk with Rabbi Davidson.
Neighbors have cockamayme ideas
about how my losses—my husband Sam,

my daughter Shelly—should make me feel.
This grief cuts jagged spirals,
but I refuse

to wallow in bitterness.
She who can't endure the bad
will not live to see the good.

My grandsons should only be well.
I pray for their father's joy.
The boys need him.

PAPÁ

El Chato habló desde las
    filipinas,
dijo que Shelly falleció.
Siento la agonía de mi hijo
como si fuera el día de la muerte
de nuestro hijo Dick.
Ese día mi madre llegó,
sintió mi dolor y se desmayó.
Ahora sufro el llanto de mi hijo
como mi madre sufrió el mío.

DAD

Chato phoned from the
    Philippines,
told of Shelly's death.
I feel my son's agony
as if it were the day
of our son Dick's death.
That day my mother arrived,
felt my grief and fainted.
Now I suffer my son's howls
as my mother suffered mine.

MOM

Chato, you phone from Baguio and say, *Shelly died yesterday in a*
   hiking accident.

I say, *I'm horrified.*
What you've suffered,
what you have yet to suffer.
I know.

I remember that day eight years ago.
I sliced an apple for your brother Dick,
went to the corner store,

came back, blood seeping
from his room, door jammed.
Your brother Bob forced the door,

a fallen chair, a pistol,
Dick on the floor.

What you've suffered,
what you have yet to suffer.

SAM

He asks me, his father, when
he will get
  a new mother.
    He sits straight, protects

his brother Manny,
pushes my hand
  that seeks to comfort.
    The shoes I chose

slid off
the crumbling trough.
  He speaks
    my unspoken thought,

says he wishes
  I had died,
    not her.

MANNY

Strangers kiss me
say sorry.

At each new place

my head turns
side to side.

I search

for what I've lost
cannot find

what's not there.

My blanket
with the smooth part

gone.

CRAZY SAVAGE

Last week, I pounded Sam.
I'm older, bigger, faster.
I slapped his face,

kicked him in the balls,
wouldn't let him give up.

Today, Sam's bruised.
He grabs my shoulder,
thuds me to the ground,

his fists hammer me.
I curl into a ball.

Dad says Sam's mom just died.
I don't believe it.
All little boys have moms,

but Dad says that's why
Sam's turned crazy savage.

BACK IN BAGUIO

I can't be a mother
for Sam and Manny,

but I hold them, feed them,
change diapers, give baths,
buy Leggos and comics,

read them to sleep with Tintin stories.
They need me, I need
their need pulling

me from bed in the morning.
Sam smiles at my sobs, tells
me to raise my glass and say cheers.

Losing a crayon
makes us weep.
I hug and the boys hug me back.

EPILOGUE

About ten months after Shelly's death our mentor, Hal Conklin, visited Mungayang with a few Ifugaos from the village where he did research. His Ifugao companions suspected foul play. They walked with Conchita Cumaldi to the spot where Shelly fell. After their visit, they were convinced that Shelly's death was accidental.

*

At fourteen months my grandson Gabo, Sam and Naima's son, has curly hair and a laugh like Manny's at that age.

Note

Shelly and I each authored a book on the Ilongots among whom we lived in Kakidguen, our home base, for three years (the two academic years of 1967–69 and the calendar year of 1974).

Shelly's book, among other things, describes oratory, a form of speech used in settling disputes. It has distinct cadences, vocabulary, and metaphors. Only a few men have the leadership and linguistic ability to orate. Her book is called *Knowledge and Passion: Ilongot Notions of Self and Social Life*. Cambridge: Cambridge University Press, 1980. See page 121 for the hunting spell in the poem, "Tepeg," and page 214 for a genealogy of Ilongots portrayed in the poems above. See also "I Have Nothing to Hide: The Language of Ilongot Oratory," *Language in Society* 2 (1973): 193–223.

My book is a history of a people who, according to many anthropologists and Philippine lowlanders, are not supposed to have one. It is called *Ilongot Headhunting, 1883–1974: A Study in Society and History*. Stanford: Stanford University Press. See also "The Story of Tukbaw: 'They Listen as He Orates'" in *The Biographical Process: Studies in the History and Psychology of Religion*, edited by Frank Reynolds and Donald Capp. The Hague: Mouton, 1976, pp. 121–51.

NOTES ON POETRY AND ETHNOGRAPHY

*

This essay provides a context for anthropological readers who are not habitual readers of poetry and who may wonder why I have written about this traumatic event in free verse rather than my once customary prose. It also constitutes, for poets, a manifesto for *antropoesía* or anthropoetry. It makes a case for poetry that situates itself in a social and cultural world; poetry that is centrally about the human condition.

The Event

The subject of this collection of poetry is an event, the death of Michelle Zimbalist Rosaldo in the Philippines. This event erupted into my life, but also into a number of other lives in the village of Mungayang and the nearby towns of Lagawe and Kiangan. This collection attempts to capture that eruption and its reverberations through the medium of poetry. For some readers the words "event" and "erupt" will bring to mind the work of the French philosopher Alain Badiou. In Badiou's thought, says Jean-Jacques Lecercle in his lucid summary, "This is an event":

> Our hero, on the road to a neighboring town, meets God. His life, and ours, are irremediably changed by the encounter. . . . The event is a violent irruption, or intervention, in an established world. This irruption, which has the force of a volcanic eruption, is also an interruption. It cancels the time of the current situation and marks a new foundation of time; the only name that aptly accounts for it is "revolution." . . . It comes and goes in a flash (it has no proper duration: its temporality is the retroactive temporality of after-the-event). (Lecercle 2002:108)

The material of poetry is not so much the raw event as the traces it leaves:

> (It interrupts and it founds), but it leaves traces, traces that allow an *encounter* with elements of the situation, who undergo a process of conviction, or conversion. Those elements become the militants (or witnesses) of the event, which has initiated a process of *truth*. The Badiou event . . . occurs in a flash, and interrupts the time of the situation; but it also founds another time, the time of the inquest, of the process of truth and faithfulness . . . — no wonder it should be a "violent gesture." . . . The highest task of literature is not to represent the event, to re-enact or reproduce in memory the flash or illumination with the Lacanian Real, but to *be* the event itself. (Lecercle 2002:108–30)

The ambition of poetry is indeed "to *be* the event itself."

The first poem I wrote about Shelly's death, "The Omen of Mungayang," initially drafted in the summer of 2000, concerns the moment I learned of Shelly's accident and ran to her body:

> Minutes later, Conchita
> steps into the hut and rasps, *She fell*
> *into the river.* I run, reach Shelly's body, drop
> to her side. A fly buzzes in, then out of her mouth.

The fly entering her mouth is a poetic image of finality — brute, traumatic. But above all it is the recollection of a harrowing experience, the moment of devastating loss, the personal realization of mortality. In the poem my sons further instruct me about mortality in ways I do not expect: "I put Sam on my shoulders, tell him his mom is dead. / He wants to know when he will get a new one."

At the time I did not expect to write more about this subject, but seven years later my poetry returned to the subject of Shelly's death. This time the poem, dedicated to my son Manuel, shows how I knew that he, even at fourteen months, was aware of his birth mother's death. The poem, "How Do I, Renato, Know That Manny Knows," portrays the infant Manny's mood — at peace, then disturbed:

Manny babbles, saying gibble, gibble,
happily cooing. Then he abruptly screeches
a piercing sound that ricochets

through the dark wooden hut
penetrating like a mouse that scurries
across smooth brown planks.

After learning of Shelly's death, I prepare to leave the village of
Mungayang: "Bags packed quickly. Conchita's cousin lifts Manny /
onto her back. He sobs, low and long. She collapses." And then,
after an eight-hour car ride:

In Baguio City I carry him into our apartment.
He searches swivels nobody here.

He bellows and shatters
the enormous thick silence.

From the remote village of Mungayang to the distant town of Ba-
guio, the poem concentrates on Manny's reactions to his birth
mother's death.

In Badiou's terms, the event produces, among the elements of
the situation, a conversion. This transformation of the subject's life
course is shown, for example, in the poem called "I Was Walking":

My steps measured
the trail visible ahead

until I flowed past the gate
as if through a funnel
to the other side

my vision gone
the gate lost behind
all changed utterly

as if my right arm gone
what most sustained me
gone.

The poem, I think, speaks for itself.

How These Poems Were Written

More than a year after composing the initial draft of "How Do I, Renato, Know That Manny Knows," I presented it for discussion at a poetry workshop. The other poets found my poem hard to follow because it had too many characters: Shelly, Renato, Sam, and Manny as well as our guide Conchita and her cousin, not to mention a soldier, a tricycle taxi driver, and a priest. (In subsequent drafts I dropped the latter three people and dedicated separate poems to each.) The workshop leader, Patricia Spears Jones, asked who the various people were and why I wanted to include them in the poem. I talked on and on, fairly bursting with things to say about the seemingly extraneous people in the poem. She then astutely observed that my verbal outpourings indicated that my poem contained the raw material for a longer series, perhaps an entire collection, but she also warned that I had stumbled onto a compelling project that would prove harrowing as a psychic space in which to dwell for the long period of composition. I was fearful of having to immerse myself in that day of trauma. I was also apprehensive about the effect of this poetic inquiry on my relations in the present, particularly with my love of many years, Mary Louise Pratt.

I was rightfully hesitant about dwelling for so long in overwhelming feelings of shock and trauma. The prospect was daunting, even some twenty-eight years after the fact. I felt apprehensive about what my poetic inquiry would uncover. What would I find in the difficult to access recesses of memory? In previous years, I did not want to write about the day of Shelly's death, but by the spring of 2009 the need to write these poems had become urgent, more an involuntary necessity than a free choice. That it took so long to begin writing on this topic, in retrospect, is not surprising. One thinks, for example, of Yusef Komunyakaa's remarkable Vietnam war poems, *Dien Cai Dau* (1988), and the fourteen years that passed before he was able to write that work. In his words: "I keep a mental notebook. I realize that I might write an image down that has reoccurred for four, five, or six years. . . . A good example is my Vietnam poems, where it's taken me about fourteen years to start getting these down" (2003:63).

I wrote the initial drafts of most of my poems in two periods of intense composition: the early summers of 2009 and 2010 when Mary Louise Pratt and I spent time at her family cottage on the Bruce Peninsula in Ontario, Canada. During the summer of 2009 I deliberately worked entirely from memory. In so doing I found that one recollection often led to another. I tried to recover details — smells, feelings, objects, words. The pathways of memory were many and, at times, uncanny. I remembered vividly, for example, my conversations with the Catholic priest who drove me and my sons the eight hours from Kiangan to Baguio. But his name eluded me. In order to draft the poem, I made up a name for him: Father Joe. Months later, when I consulted my field journal, I found that his name was indeed Father Joe.

By the summer of 2010 I consulted my field journal, which I had kept in the Philippines up to the day of Shelly's death. After arriving home, I resumed my journal, backwriting from the day I had stopped and continued writing until the following January. I found that my memory and my field journal supplemented one another. At times I remembered incidents that I had neglected to record in my journal. At other times I failed to recall names, places, or incidents and found them there. No doubt there were things I neither recalled nor recorded in my journal, but, of course, I have no knowledge of what I've forgotten.

The Work of Poetry

The work of poetry, as I practice it in this collection, is to bring its subject — whether pain, sorrow, shock, or joy — home to the reader. It is not an ornament; it does not make things pretty. Nor does it shy away from agony and distress. Instead it brings things closer, or into focus, or makes them palpable. It slows the action, the course of events, to reveal depth of feeling and to explore its character. It is a place to dwell and savor more than a space for quick assessment.

Poetic exploration resembles ethnographic inquiry in that insight emerges from specifics more than from generalizations. In neither case do concrete particulars illustrate an already formulated theory. In antropoesía, my term (in Spanish) for verse informed by an ethnographic sensibility, I strive for accuracy and engage in forms of inquiry where I am surprised by the unexpected. Antropoesía is a process of discovery more than a confirmation of the already known. If one knows precisely where a poem is going before beginning to write there is no point in going further. The same can be said of thick description in ethnography where theory is to be discovered in the details. The details inspire theory rather than illustrate already formulated theory.

Antropoesía, verse with an ethnographic sensibility, designates poetry where description is central. A poet who articulates this perspective is the late New York writer, Harvey Shapiro, who spoke of himself as being, "very loosely," an objectivist. Being an objectivist, for him, "is a belief in the healing power that resides in the eye's ability to see the world. . . . It's the belief that words don't point to words but that words point to real things in the world. It's the opposite of the Language Poets" (Williams 2001:4). Shapiro distinguishes these two poles—words that point to words versus words that point to the world—in order to differentiate two schools of poetry: the Objectivists as opposed to the Language Poets. In my view his distinction more usefully underscores a tension inherent in all poetry, that between striving for the music or magic of language and seeking to explore the world—nature, politics, society, psyche. In my verse I attend to language, but I do not try to replicate a person's speech as if I were a recording device. Nor do I believe that representation is transparent or that a correspondence theory of meaning is valid. Instead I seek telling details that characterize a person or a revealing phrase of everyday speech that transcends by being luminous, ominous, or, perhaps, uncanny.

In this vein poets may speak, perhaps with irony, of the poetry of mere description. Consider B. H. Fairchild's "The Machinist, Teaching His Daughter to Play the Piano": "The brown wrist and hand with its raw knuckles and blue nails / packed with dirt and oil, pause in mid-air, / the fingers arched delicately" (1998:30). Or consider "Sunday in the Empty Nest" by Sharon Olds: "Slowly it strikes me how quiet it is. / It's deserted at our house. There's no one here, / no one needing anything of us / and no one will need anything of us / for months" (2002:53). Or consider Juan Felipe Herrera's "19 Pokrovskaya Street": "My father lights the kerosene lamp, his beard bitten, hand / wet from the river, where he kneels to pray in the mornings, / he sits and pulls out his razor, rummages through a gunnysack" (2008:300).

These poems create deep feeling through the accumulation of concrete particulars rather than by beginning (as so many fine lyric poets do) with a named subjective state and elaborating through image and metaphor. Like an ethnographer, the antropoeta looks and looks, listens and listens, until she sees or hears what she did not apprehend at first. This form of inquiry resembles field research in that it involves observation, asking questions, attending with patience and care, knowing that meaning may be there, waiting to be found, even if the observer-poet does not yet know what it is.

Poetry has proven compelling for me because it allows me to dwell in powerful experiences and perceptions. It enables me to render these feelings intelligible, vivid, and present. In lyric moments, I seek the larger significance in these telling details. My task, however, is not to give clarity to feelings that are in fact unclear. In the initial moment of shock, which I depict in the poems collected here, my feelings were as ill-defined as they were overwhelming. My verse does not try to transform the ill-defined into the well-defined. My task, as a poet, is to render intelligible what is complex and to bring home to the reader the uneven and contradictory shape of that moment.

I attempt to convey a yes and a no, to hold opposing forces together, making both present. I do not emphasize one pole so greatly as to erase or diminish the other. In this collection there is, to begin, the tension between absorbing devastating loss and the urgency of caring for my sons, Sam and Manny. There is, also, the tension between chronology (the press of "what happens next") and dwelling in a specific incident. There is, finally, the tension between the transformation I was undergoing and the practical imperatives of the moment.

An Accidental Field of Relations

The poems in this collection explore the subjectivities of people I encountered on that day of trauma, the day of Shelly's death. We all were affected, though differently, by Shelly's death. In writing about the people I encountered—people who for the most part I barely knew or had never met—I learned how deeply my feelings resonated within and were shaped by a field of accidental social relations. The people in this field into which I was thrown were various in their attitudes toward me: attentive, caring, aggressive, inappropriate, mixed. That there were so many people toward the caring end of this spectrum is more than I could have dared hope. I am still grateful.

The prose poem "In a White Cubicle" explores something of the range of these relations, beginning with the inappropriate:

> At the clinic in Lagawe strangers form a crowd and stare at me. One man with a cheery smile asks, *How did it happen?* The room fades to very white.

Help comes to me by grace, without my asking:

> A woman from the pharmacy asks for the American. I nod. She hands me diapers, sodas, snacks, and mosquito nets.

A local mayor proves brutal in his not unjustified reprimand:

> The Mayor of Lagawe shouts, *How could you allow your wife to walk the trail alone? Why don't you embalm the body here in Lagawe?*

And caring help comes uncalled when I desperately need it:

> Father George says, *Never mind the Mayor, he's drunk*, then drives me and the boys to the convent in a vw bug.

The local clinic was public and, for me, socially turbulent.

Through particular poems I explore the quality and impact of individuals in my field of accidental relations. I also inquire into my feelings as refracted through the perceptions of these others. From one poem to the next I change focus, subject matter, mood, and tone. I often speak for other people in their first-person voices. This approach has its risks, particularly projection—the imposition of one's perceptions on others. Yet these social relations, however accidental and fleeting they may have been, were vivid and significant. I learned from them. My account here is thus more intersubjective than purely subjective, more the result of an inquiry from a man embedded in a field of accidental social relations than a report from the lone participant observer. Consider the following poems about a soldier, a tricycle taxi driver, and a priest.

"The Soldier" shows a man displaced and at risk in Kiangan where he's been assigned: "Tourists visit rice terraces infested, / guerrilla cadres, New People's Army. / To them my ears cut off / as much a trophy as my ArmaLite." At gunpoint, the soldier orders me to stop, then observes me:

He's pale, trembling, trudging,
with him two sons, a little boy and a baby.
In him I see
the same
ashen face
knotted shoulders
automaton walk
as my father
the day my mother died.
The same.

In his eyes, I am at risk, vulnerable, caring for my sons, in a state of shock, shoulders knotted. This much the soldier can see, but at the time I cannot. He is my mirror. I'm numb and simply trying to stay on my feet. It's far too soon for me to reflect on the rage in bereavement.

In "The Tricycle Taxi Driver" the driver is waiting for me. He has heard of Shelly's death and knows I'll walk the road where he is parked. The poem begins and ends with his saying: "*Please accept my gift.*" He takes pride in his work: "In Lagawe I own the only / tricyle taxi, orange, yellow, red, / fresh paint, curving lines." Not unlike the soldier, the tricycle taxi driver observes my state of exhaustion and devastation:

The American man shoulders

his five-year-old son,
his walk heavy, shirt soaked,
face streaked with dirt,

his tears behind red eyes,

I offer to pay for the ride, but the driver says again that he wants no pay: "*Please accept my gift.*" In fact it was not until I wrote the poem that I received the blessing of the tricycle taxi driver's gift. I am deeply grateful.

My poem "Father Joe" depicts the Catholic priest who drove me, Sam, and Manny the eight hours from Kiangan to Baguio. His perceptions of Shelly and me are more intellectually inflected than those of the soldier and the tricycle taxi driver:

> I know Renato and Shelly.
> They're progressive.
> Faith in the people
> makes critical anthropology
> like my liberation theology.

He feels the loss: "I ache with Shelly's death, / barely knew her, / but the loss is bitter." I ask Father Joe for his words of wisdom: "Renato asks what there is to say. / No words, I say, no words."

Let the Scaffolding Stand

Let me now stand back from individual poems to reflect on the collection as a whole. I'd like to underline a striking fact about our arrival in Ifugao country. Shelly and I reached Mungayang for the first time late in the afternoon on the day before her death. We had never been there before. Thus my poems depict our first (and only) day of field research. We hoped to live in Mungayang and do fieldwork for a couple of months during the following summer. In Baguio, a large town eight hours from Ifugao country, where we were teaching on a Fulbright grant, we started to study the language with native speakers studying there. At the time we understood little and spoke only a few words of Ifugao, as one would expect at the very beginning of a field research project. My collection of poems makes central the kinds of people who are placed off-stage in most ethnographies—a tricycle taxi driver and a soldier as well as priests and nuns whose hospitality I depended upon utterly. I entrusted myself and my sons to their care. I owe them an incalculable debt.

The exclusion from most ethnographies of the kinds of people who figure so prominently in this collection of poems reveals the undisclosed infrastructure of such work. This exclusion has a long tradition, not only in ethnography, but also in travel writing and natural history. In *Imperial Eyes*, Mary Louise Pratt notes that Alexander von Humboldt, for example, relied on the hospitality and logistical support of the colonial society in order to reinvent South America as primal nature:

> Despite the emphasis on primal nature, in all their explorations, Humboldt and Bonpland never once stepped beyond the boundaries of the Spanish colonial infrastructure—they couldn't, for they relied entirely on the networks of villages, missions, outposts, haciendas, roadways, and colonial labor systems to sustain themselves and their project, for food, shelter, and the labor pool to guide them and transport their immense equipage. (1992:127)

In his early and most influential writings, however, Humboldt removes his hosts from view. Nor does he ask to what extent his observations were conditioned and shaped by them. Similarly, ethnographic inquiry is haunted by categories of persons who inhabit the sites of field research, but are rarely depicted by anthropologists. Eliminated from view, as they often are, these people have an invisible presence and occasionally make a shadowy appearance in the acknowledgments or a preface.

In my previous Philippine field research, for example, I devoted myself to learning Ilongot, but never learned Ilocano, the trade language of the region. It was the mother tongue of the local mayor, police, traders, and other visitors from nearby towns and villages to the settlement where Shelly and I lived for three years. I had no difficulty conversing, however, with New Tribes evangelical Christian missionaries, Americans and Filipinos, who were in residence among the Ilongots. They had been there for more than fifteen years. We spoke often and on many topics. Shelly and I flew in their Piper Cubs and stayed in their homes, including a few extended visits when stranded by typhoons. Though I neither conducted formal interviews about their beliefs and practices nor attempted an oral history of their work in the region, our lengthy conversations deeply instructed me about their lives and their work. I also read what the American missionaries residing among the Ilongots wrote about their activities in the New Tribes magazines, *Island Challenge* and *Brown Gold*. They were a powerful force for social change in the region. Yet our ethnography on the Ilongots never analyzed the presence and impact of these New Tribes missionaries.

The elimination of certain people from ethnography can be accounted for by what Bruno Latour in *We Have Never Been Modern* calls the "purification" of science. Classic ethnography calls for a purified object of study, a circumscribed culture or society. All other people, even those who reside with and have an impact on members of the culture being studied, are excluded from view. In this now-dated schema, ethnographers are the ones who move and natives are the ones who stay in their ancestral habitat. The heroics of ethnography require a solitary observer who can focus exclusively on the objects of study.

In this schema of ethnographic research, nonnatives, even those living on native lands, are extraneous. They include such people as local-level state functionaries, doctors, nurses, teachers, police, soldiers, petty merchants, drivers, miners, contract workers, and missionaries. Yet most ethnographers, soon after they reach their research sites, seek out these kinds of people and rely on them for logistical support and an initial orientation to the people and the place. Nonetheless, nonnatives in native lands are scaffolding, crucial for the phase of construction, but destined to be torn down and removed once the ethnographic edifice has been built. In my experience, when the ethnographic mission collapsed, this scaffolding remained standing, rich and complex, in plain view. There, the net into which I fell.

Note

I am indebted for comments on this essay to Mary Louise Pratt and to people who asked questions after I presented earlier versions of this essay at The University of Melbourne, Australia, The University of Texas at Austin, and a faculty colloquium in the Department of Social and Cultural Analysis at New York University.

Anthropologists who are also poets usually trace our genealogies to the eminent ancestors Edward Sapir and Ruth Benedict. Benedict published her poetry under the name Anne Singleton. (For samples of their poetry and their correspondence about poetry, see Margaret Mead, *An Anthropologist at Work: Writings of Ruth Benedict* [New York: Avon Books, 1959].) Other notable predecessors include Paul Friedrich and Dell Hymes. More recently a number of anthropologists have written verse and written about verse in other cultures. Among them are Jerome Rothenberg, Dennis Tedlock, Lila Abu-Lughod, and Ivan Brady. To bring this incomplete list more up-to-date I would add Ruth Behar, Melisa Cahnmann-Taylor, Valentine Daniel, Michael Jackson, Adrie Kusserow, Kent Maynard, and Nomi Stone. The Society for Humanistic Anthropology sponsors panels, readings, and workshops for these and other poets as well as noted ethnographic writers of memoir and fiction at the annual meetings of the American Anthropological Association.

Works Cited

Fairchild, B. F. 1998. "The Machinist, Teaching His Daughter to Play the Piano." *The Art of the Lathe*. Farmington, ME: Alice James Books.

Herrera, Juan Felipe. 2008. "19 Pokrovskaya Street." *Half of the World in Light: New and Selected Poems*. Tucson: The University of Arizona Press.

Komunyakaa, Yusef. 1988. *Dien Cai Dau*. Hanover, NH: Wesleyan University Press.

———. 2000. *Blue Notes: Essays, Interviews, and Commentaries*. Ann Arbor: The University of Michigan Press.

Latour, Bruno. 1993. *We Have Never Been Modern*. Cambridge: Harvard University Press.

Lecercle, Jean-Jacques. 2002. *Deleuze and Language*. New York: Palgrave Macmillan.

Olds, Sharon. 2002. "Sunday in the Empty Nest." *The Unswept Room*. New York: Alfred A. Knopf.

Pratt, Mary Louise. 1992. *Imperial Eyes: Travel Writing and Transculturation*. London: Routledge.

Williams, Galen. 2001. Poetic Lives I: Harvey Shapiro, in conversation with Galen Williams. www.brooklynrail.org/2001/08/poetic-lives-i-harvey-shapiro-in-conversation-with-galen-williams.

PART II

*

GRIEF AND A HEADHUNTER'S RAGE

*

On the Cultural Force of Emotions

In what follows I discuss how to talk about the cultural force of emotions. *Emotional force* refers to the kinds of feelings one experiences on learning, for example, that the child just run over by a car is one's own and not a stranger's. One must consider, in other words, the subject's position within a field of social relations in order to grasp their emotional experience. This approach of showing the force of a simple statement taken literally instead of explicating culture through the gradual thickening of symbolic webs of meaning can widen our discipline's theoretical range. The vocabulary for symbolic analysis, in other words, can expand by adding the term *force* to more familiar concepts, such as *thick description, multivocality, polysemy, richness,* and *texture.*[1] The notion of force, among other things, opens to question the common assumption that the greatest human import always resides in the densest forest of symbols and that cultural depth always equals cultural elaboration. Do people always, in fact, describe most thickly what to them matters most?

If you ask an older Ilongot man of northern Luzon, Philippines, why he cuts off human heads, his answer is a one-liner, on which no anthropologist can really elaborate: he says that rage, born of grief, impels him to kill his fellow human beings. The act of severing and tossing away the victim's head enables him, he says, to vent and hopefully throw away the anger of his bereavement. The job of cultural analysis, then, is to make this man's statement plausible and comprehensible. Yet further questioning reveals that he has little more to say about the connections between bereavement, rage, and headhunting, connections that seem so powerful to him as to be self-evident beyond explication. Either you understand it or you don't. And, in fact, for the longest time I simply did not.

It was not until some fourteen years after first recording this simple statement about grief and a headhunter's rage that I began to grasp its overwhelming force. For years I thought that more verbal elaboration (which was not forthcoming) or another analytical level (which remained elusive) could better explain the kinds of things these older men, when enraged by grief, can do to their fellow human beings. It was not until I was repositioned through lived experience that I became better able to grasp that Ilongot older men mean precisely what they say when they describe the anger in bereavement as the source of their desire to cut off human heads. This statement, taken at face value and granted its full weight, reveals much about how Ilongots can find headhunting so compelling.

The Rage in Ilongot Grief

The Ilongots number some 3,500. Living in an upland area some 150 km northeast of Manila, they subsist by hunting deer and wild pig and by cultivating rain-fed gardens (swiddens) and rice, sweet potatoes, manioc, and vegetables. Their kin relations are bilateral. Due to the fact that upon marriage the husband moves into his wife's home (uxorilocal postmarital residence), parents and their married daughters live in the same or adjacent households. Sibling ties among married couples in the senior generation link the dispersed houses within local clusters. The largest unit within the society, a largely territorial putative descent group called the bērtan, is manifest primarily in the context of headhunting feuds. Headhunting, for themselves, for their neighbors, and for their ethnographers, stands out as the Ilongots' most salient cultural practice.

When Ilongots told me, as they often did, how the rage in bereavement could impel men to headhunt, I brushed aside their one-line accounts as too simple, thin, opaque, implausible, stereotypic, or otherwise unsatisfying. Probably, I was naïvely equating grief with sadness. Certainly no personal experience allowed me to imagine the force of rage possible in bereavement for older Ilongot men. Such seemingly simple Ilongot statements thus led me to seek out another level of analysis that could provide deeper explanations for the older men's desire to headhunt.

In a representative foray along these lines, I pursued the deeper explanation by trying to use exchange theory, perhaps because it had informed so many celebrated ethnographies, to solve the analytical problem. One day in 1974, I explained the anthropologist's model to an older Ilongot man named Insan. What did he think, I asked, of the idea that headhunting resulted from one death (the beheaded victim's) cancelling another (the next of kin). He looked puzzled, so I went on to say that the victim of a beheading was exchanged for one's own dead kin, thereby, so to speak, balancing the books. Insan reflected on this for a moment and then replied that he imagined somebody could think such a thing (a safe bet, since I just had) but that he and other Ilongots did not think any such thing. Nor was there any indirect evidence for my exchange theory in ritual, boast, song, or casual conversation.[2]

In retrospect, then, these efforts to impose exchange theory on one aspect of Ilongot behavior appear feeble. Suppose I had discovered what I sought? Although the notion of balancing the ledger does have a certain elegant coherence, one wonders why such bookish dogma could inspire any man to take another man's life at the risk of his own.

My life experience had as yet not provided the means to imagine the rage that can come with devastating loss. Nor could I therefore fully appreciate the acute problem of meaning that Ilongots faced in 1974. Shortly after Ferdinand Marcos declared martial law in 1972, rumors reached the Ilongot hills that firing squads had become the new punishment for headhunting. In past epochs when headhunting had become impossible, Ilongots had allowed their rage to dissipate in the course of everyday life as best they could. In 1974, they instead began to consider conversion to Evangelical Christianity as an alternative means of coping with their grief. Accepting the new religion, people said, implied abandoning their old ways, including headhunting. It also made coping with bereavement less agonizing because they could believe that the deceased had departed for a better world. No longer did they have to confront the awful finality of death.

The force of the dilemma faced by Ilongots at that time eluded me. Even when I correctly recorded their statements about grieving and the need to throw away their anger, I simply did not grasp the weight of their words. In 1974, for example, while Michelle Rosaldo and I were living among the Ilongots, a six-month-old baby died, probably of pneumonia. That afternoon we visited the father and found him terribly stricken: "He was sobbing and staring through glazed and bloodshot eyes at the cotton blanket" covering his dead baby (R. Rosaldo 1980:286). The man suffered intensely, for this was the seventh child he had lost. Just a few years before, three of his children had died, one after the other, in a matter of days. At the time, the situation was murky as people present talked both about Evangelical Christianity and about their grudges against lowlanders as they expressed their anger and perhaps contemplated headhunting forays into the surrounding valleys.

Through subsequent days and weeks, however, the man's grief moved him in a way I had not anticipated. Shortly after the baby's death the father converted to Evangelical Christianity. Altogether too quick on the inference, I immediately concluded that the man believed that the new religion could somehow prevent further deaths in his family. When I pursued this line of thought, an Ilongot friend sharply corrected me, saying that

> I had missed the point: what the man in fact sought in the new religion was not the denial of our inevitable deaths, but a means of coping with his grief. With the advent of Martial Law, headhunting was out of the question as a means of venting his wrath and thereby lessening his grief. Were he to remain in his Ilongot way of life, the pain of his sorrow would simply be too much to bear. (R. Rosaldo 1980:288)

Taken verbatim from my own monograph, this description now seems so apt that I wonder how I nonetheless could have failed to appreciate the weight and power of the man's desire for "venting his wrath and thereby lessening his grief."

Another anecdote makes all more remarkable this failure to imagine the rage possible in Ilongot bereavement. On this occasion Michelle Rosaldo and I were urged by Ilongot friends to play the tape of a headhunting celebration we had witnessed some five years earlier. No sooner had we turned on the tape recorder and heard the boast of a man who had died in the intervening years than did people abruptly tell us to shut off the machine. Michelle Rosaldo (1980:33) reported on the tense conversation that ensued:

As Insan braced himself to speak, the room again became almost uncannily electric. Backs straightened and my anger turned to nervousness and something more like fear as I saw that Insan's eyes were red. Tukbaw, Renato's Ilongot "brother," then broke into what was a brittle silence, saying he could make things clear. He told us that it hurt to listen to a headhunting celebration when people knew that there would never be another. As he put it: "The song pulls at us, drags our hearts, it makes us think of our dead uncle." And again: "It would be different if I had accepted God, but I still am an Ilongot at heart; and when I hear the song, my heart aches as it does when I must look upon unfinished bachelors whom I know that I will never lead to take a head." Then Wagat, Tukbaw's wife, said with her eyes that all my questions gave her pain, and told me: "Leave off now, isn't that enough? Even I, a woman, cannot stand the way it feels inside my heart."

From my present position it now is evident that the tape recording with the dead man's boast spontaneously revived among those listening powerful feelings of bereavement, particular rage, and the impulse to headhunt. At the time I could only be frightened and sense the force of the emotions experienced by Tukbaw, Insan, Wagat, and the others present.

The dilemma for Ilongots grew out of a set of cultural practices that, when blocked, were agonizing to live with. This blockage called for painful adjustments to other modes of experiencing their bereavement. One could compare this dilemma with Alfred Radcliffe-Brown's notion that ritual, particularly when not performed, can create anxiety. In this case, the Ilongot cultural notion that to throw away a human head is also to cast away the anger in one's grief creates a problem of meaning when headhunting is out of the question. What, then, is a man to do with the anger in his grief? Indeed, the classic Weberian problem of meaning is precisely of this kind. On a logical plane the doctrine of predestination seems flawless: God has chosen the elect but his decision can never be known by mortals. If a group's ultimate concern is salvation, however, this coherent doctrine proves impossible to live with for all but the religious virtuoso. The problem of meaning, for Calvinists and Ilongots alike, involves practice, not theory. At stake for both groups are practical matters concerning how to live with one's beliefs, rather than logical puzzlement produced by an abstract doctrine.

How I Found the Rage in Grief

One burden of this essay concerns the claim that it took some fourteen years for me to grasp what Ilongots had told me about their grief, rage, and headhunting. During all those years I was not yet in a position to comprehend the force of anger possible in bereavement, and now I am. Introducing myself into this account requires a certain hesitation both because of the discipline's taboo and because of its increasingly frequent violation by essays laced with trendy amalgams of continental philosophy and autobiographical snippets. The vice of the latter trend, of course, is that reflexivity leads the self-absorbed Self to lose sight altogether of the Other. Despite this risk, as the ethnographer I must enter the discussion at this point to elucidate certain issues of method.

The key concept in what follows is that of the positioned (and repositioned) subject. In routine interpretive procedure, according to the methodology of hermeneutics, one can say that ethnographers reposition themselves as they go about understanding other cultures. One begins with a set of questions and subsequently revises them in the course of inquiry. Thus, ethnographers emerge from fieldwork with a different set of questions than those they posed on initial entry. Ask a question, in other words, and through surprise at the answer you'll revise your questions until lessening surprises or diminishing returns indicates a stopping point. This approach has been most influentially articulated within anthropology by Clifford Geertz (1974).

The view of interpretive method usually rests on the axiom that gifted ethnographers learn their trade through a broad course of preparation. In order to follow the meandering course of ethnographic inquiry, fieldworkers require wide-ranging theoretical capacities and finely tuned sensibilities. After all, one cannot predict beforehand what one will encounter in the field. Clyde Kluckhohn even went so far as to recommend a double initiation: first the ordeal of psychoanalysis and then that of fieldwork. All too often, this view is extended so that certain prerequisites of actual field research appear to guarantee an authoritative ethnography. Eclectic book knowledge and a range of life experiences, edifying reading and self-awareness, supposedly vanquish the twin vices of ignorance and insensitivity.

Although the doctrine of preparation, knowledge, and sensibility contains much to admire, one should work to undermine the false comfort it can convey. At what point, for example, can people say that they have completed their learning or their life experience? The problem with taking too much to heart this mode of preparing the ethnographer is that it can lend a false air of security, an authoritative claim to certitude and finality that our analyses cannot have: All interpretations are provisional; they are made by positioned subjects who are prepared to know certain things and not others. Good ethnographers, knowledgeable and sensitive, fluent in the language, and able to move easily in an alien cultural world, still have their limits and their analyses always are incomplete. Thus, I began to fathom the force of what Ilongots had been telling me about their losses through the accident of my own devastating loss and not through any systematic preparation for field research.

My own understanding had been prepared a little over a decade earlier with my brother's death in 1970. By experiencing this agonizing ordeal with my mother and father, I gained a measure of insight into the trauma of a parent losing a child. This insight informed my account, partially described earlier, of an Ilongot man's reactions to the death of his seventh child. At the same time, my bereavement was so much less than that of my parents that I could not then imagine the overwhelming force of rage possible in such grief. My not having known the depth of rage possible in grief is rather general in the discipline. Ethnographic knowledge has the strengths and limitations given by the relative youth of most fieldworkers who, for example, have no personal knowledge of how devastating the loss of a long-term partner can be for the survivor.

In 1981 Michelle Rosaldo and I began field research among the Ifugaos of northern Luzon, Philippines. On October 11 of that year, Shelly was walking along a trail with two Ifugao companions when she lost her footing and fell to her death some 20 m down a sheer precipice into the swollen river below. Immediately on finding her body I became enraged. How could she abandon me? How could she have been so stupid as to fall? I tried to cry. I sobbed, but rage blocked the tears. Earlier lived experience, on the fourth anniversary of my brother's death, had taught me to recognize heaving sobs without tears as a form of anger. This anger, in a number of forms, has swept over me on many occasions since Shelly's death, lasting hours and even days at a time. Such feelings can be aroused by rituals, but more often they emerge from unexpected reminders (not unlike the Ilongots' experience of their dead uncle's recorded voice).

Lest there be any misunderstanding, bereavement should not be reduced to anger, neither for myself nor for anyone else. Powerful visceral emotional states swept over me, at times separately and at other times together. Among other things, I felt in my chest the deep cutting pain of sorrow almost beyond endurance, the cadaverous cold of realizing the finality of death, the trembling beginning in my abdomen and spreading through my body as a form of wailing, the mournful keening that started without my willing, and frequent tearful sobbing. My present purpose of revising earlier understandings of Ilongot headhunting and not a general view of bereavement thus grants centrality to the anger rather than the other emotions in grief.

I should probably add that writings in English especially need to emphasize the emotion of anger. Although grief therapists routinely encourage awareness of the anger in bereavement, American culture in general ignores the rage that devastating losses can bring. Paradoxically, cultural wisdom denies the anger in grief even though members of the invisible community of the bereaved can be encouraged to talk obsessively about their anger. My brother's death in combination with Ilongot teachings about anger (for them, a publicly celebrated rather than a hidden emotion) allowed me immediately to recognize the experience of rage.

Writing in my journal some six weeks after Shelly's death, I noted: "If I ever return to anthropology by writing 'Grief and a Headhunter's Rage. . . .'" It seems, as I discovered only a week before completing the initial draft of this essay, that I had made a vow to myself about how I would return, if I did so, to writing anthropology. Reflecting further on death, rage, and headhunting, my journal goes on to describe my "wish for the Ilongot solution; they are much more in touch with reality than Christians. So, I need a place to carry my anger—and can we say a solution of the imagination is better than theirs? And can we condemn them when we napalm villages? Is our rationale so much sounder than theirs?" All this was written in despair and rage.

This essay itself, in fact, has been cathartic, though perhaps not in the way one would imagine. Not until some fifteen months after Michelle's death was I again able to begin writing anthropology. In the month before beginning this essay, I was ill with a fever and felt diffusely depressed. Then one day an almost literal fog lifted and words began to flow. Thus, the experience of catharsis enabled the writing to proceed, rather than the reverse.

By invoking personal experience as an analytical category one risks easy dismissal. Unsympathetic readers could reduce this essay to an act of mourning or to a report on a personal discovery of the anger possible in bereavement. Frankly, this essay is both and more. An act of mourning *and* a personal report, it simultaneously involves a number of distinguishable processes, no one of which cancels out the others. Indeed, in what follows I make precisely this argument about ritual in general and Ilongot headhunting in particular. The paramount claim made here, aside from revising the ethnographic record, concerns the way in which my own mourning and consequent reflection on Ilongot bereavement, rage, and headhunting raise methodological issues of general concern in anthropology.

Death in Anthropology

Symbolic anthropology in particular has privileged interpretations that ground their understanding in cultural elaboration and deeper levels of analysis. In practice, many analyses favor restricted spheres where formal and repetitive events take center stage. Consider, for example, Victor Turner on ritual process or Clifford Geertz on deep play in the Balinese cockfight. Studies of word play, in the same vein, are more likely to focus on jokes as programmed monologues than on the less-scripted, more free-wheeling improvised interchanges of witty banter. Symbolic anthropology often focuses on rituals, ceremonies, games, and other activities played out in visibly bounded arenas. These events have definite locations in space, with centers and outer edges. Temporally, they also are well defined, with fixed beginnings, middles, and endings. Historically, they appear to repeat identical structures by seemingly doing things today as they were done yesterday. Their qualities of fixed definition liberate such events from the untidiness of everyday life so that they can be "read" like articles, books, or, as we now say, *texts*.

These remarks can take on more substance in the context of particular studies of death and its rituals. Take, for example, William Douglas's book, *Death in Murelaga: Funerary Ritual in a Spanish Basque Village* (1969). Notice that the title equates death and "funerary ritual." The objective, Douglas (1969:209) says, is to use death and funerary ritual "as a heuristic device with which to approach the study of rural Basque society." The author begins his analysis by saying that "death is not always fortuitous or unpredictable" (1969:19). He goes on to describe how an old woman, ailing with the infirmities of her age, welcomed her death. The description itself largely ignores the perspective of the most bereaved survivors and instead vacillates between those of the old woman and a detached observer.

Undeniably, certain people do live a full life and suffer so greatly in their decrepitude that they can embrace the relief death can bring. Yet the problem with making an ethnography's major case study focus on "a very easy death" (I use Simone de Beauvoir's title with irony, as she did) is not only its lack of representativeness but also that it makes death in general appear as routine for the survivors as this particular one apparently was for the deceased. Were the old woman's sons and daughters untouched by her death? The case study shows less about how people cope with death than about how death can be made to appear routine, thereby fitting neatly into the author's view of funerary ritual as a mechanical programmed unfolding of prescribed acts. "To the Basque," says Douglas (1969:75), "ritual is order and order is ritual."

Putting the accent on the routine aspects of ritual conveniently conceals the agony of such unexpected early deaths as parents losing a grown child or a mother dying in childbirth. Concealed in such descriptions are the agonies of the survivors who muddle through shifting, powerful emotional states. Although Douglas acknowledges the distinction between the bereaved members of the deceased's domestic group and the more public ritualistic group, he writes his account primarily from the viewpoint of the latter. He masks the emotional forces of bereavement by reducing funerary ritual to orderly routine.

In a more recent compendium of the wisdom of the discipline, Richard Huntington and Peter Metcalf's *Celebration of Death: The Anthropology of Mortuary Ritual* (1979) takes another tack in dismissing the presence of emotions. They admit the presence of emotions but deny their extraordinary power for understanding ritual in lines of argument made classic by Emile Durkheim and Claude Lévi-Strauss. Their argument begins by using Radcliffe-Brown to assert that "crying at funerals is not merely tolerated, it is required by custom, and at predetermined moments the entire body of mourners will burst into loud and piercing cries. Just as suddenly, weeping halts and the tears that had been running so profusely cease" (Huntingon and Metcalf 1979:24). They go on to applaud Radcliffe-Brown's notion that "the sentiment does not create the act, but wailing at the prescribed moment and in the prescribed manner creates within the wailer the proper sentiment" (1979:26). Thus far, the argument on emotions seems as standard as it is sensible, but note well that conventional wisdom defines ritual and obligatory behavior as one and the same. Collapsing the two eliminates the space for improvisation and spontaneous sentiment within ritual.[3]

When Huntington and Metcalf discuss Durkheim, they extend their argument on ritual weeping by saying, "We cannot assume that people actually feel the sorrow they express" (1979:31). Certainly, the obligatory acts of ritual do not arise from spontaneous sentiment, but neither should one assume that people do or do not "feel the sorrow they express." One could reasonably assume, along these lines, that certain people just go through the motions while other people's ritual wailing is heartfelt. Even here, however, one could not simply say that those most attached to the deceased most feel the emotions they express, whereas those most distant least feel them. A death can touch one deeply because of its resonance with other personal losses, rather than because of one's intimate ties with the deceased. The point, in any case, is that analysis can assume neither that individuals do nor do not feel the sentiments they express during a funeral.

Huntington and Metcalf complete their dismissal of emotions in mortuary ritual by saying, "Though often intense, emotional reactions to death are too varied and shifting to provide the foundation for a theory of mortuary ritual" (1979:44). Thus far I am with them, but they go on:

> The need to release aggression, or break ties with the deceased or complete any other putatively universal psychic process, does not serve to explain funerals. The shoe is on the other foot. Whatever mental adjustments the individual needs to make in the face of death he or she must accomplish as best he or she can, through such rituals as society provides. (1979:44)

Their claim that "in the face of death" individuals rely entirely on "such rituals as society provides" makes a crucial mistake: it collapses the ritual process and the process of mourning.

Surely, human beings mourn both in ritual settings and in the informal settings of everyday life. Consider, for example, the following passage from a paper by Godfrey Wilson that Huntington and Metcalf cite:

> That some at least of those who attend a Nyakyusa burial are moved by grief it is easy to establish. I have heard people talking regretfully in ordinary conversation of a man's death; I have seen a man whose sister had just died walk over alone towards her grave and weep quietly by himself without any parade of grief; and I have heard of a man killing himself because of his grief for a dead son. (Wilson 1939:22–23)

Note that all the instances Wilson has witnessed happened outside the circumscribed sphere of ritual where people simply conversed among themselves, walked alone, or, more impulsively, committed suicide. The work of grieving, probably universally, occurs both within obligatory ritual acts and in more everyday settings where people find themselves alone or with close kin.

The general argument that Huntington and Metcalf make can easily be turned on its head. Just as the intense emotions of bereavement do not explain obligatory ritual acts, so obligatory ritual acts do not explain the intense emotions of bereavement. It is no more true that all intense emotional states are obligatory (as Huntington and Metcalf seem to claim) than to assert that all obligatory emotional states are intense. The approach to ritual advocated by these authors works to deny the socially consequential force of emotions that can overwhelm the bereaved, especially the chief mourners. Even in the face of volatile rage and sorrow, such analyses allow the comfort of denial through their focus on the elegant order often found in prescribed cultural elaboration.

Among the Nyakyusa, to return to Wilson's account, men danced with the passions of their bereavement. They described their feelings in this manner:

"This war dance (*ukukina*)," said an old man, "is mourning, we are mourning the dead man. We dance because there is war in our hearts. A passion of grief and fear exasperates us (*ilyyojo likutusila*)." . . . *Elyojo* means a passion or grief, anger or fear; *ukusila* means to annoy or exasperate beyond endurance. In explaining *ukusila* one man put it like this: "If a man continually insults me then he exasperates me (*ukusila*) so that I want to fight him." Death is a fearful and grievous event that exasperates those men nearly concerned and makes them want to fight. (1939:13)

Descriptions of the dance and subsequent quarrels, even killings, provide ample evidence of the emotional intensity involved. The articulate testimony by Wilson's informants makes it obvious that even the most intense sentiments can be studied by ethnographers (see M. Rosaldo 1980).

Whether resulting from notions of objectivity or dogmas about the indeterminacy of inner states, ethnographies that eliminate such qualities as anger, lust, and tenderness both distort their descriptions and remove potentially key variables from their explanations. My use of personal experience as a point of departure in characterizing the rage of grief for Ilongots has been, among other things, a vehicle for enabling readers to apprehend the force of emotions in another culture. Ilongot anger and my own, of course, only overlap in a significant respect but they are not identical. Fantasies about life insurance agents who refused to recognize Shelly's death as job related did not, for example, lead me to kill them, cut off their heads, and celebrate afterward. Stating in such concrete terms the modest truism that any two human groups must have certain things in common can appear to fly in the face of a once-healthy methodological caution that warns against the reckless attribution of one's own categories and experiences to members of another culture. Such warnings against facile notions of universal human nature can be carried too far and harden into the equally pernicious doctrine that, my own group aside, everything human is alien to me.

Thus, in most anthropological studies of death, analysts simply eliminate emotions by assuming the position of the most detached observer. Their stance also equates the ritual with the obligatory, ignores the relation between ritual and everyday life, and conflates the ritual process with the process of mourning. The general rule, despite such exceptions as Wilson's account, seems to be that one should tidy things up as much as possible by wiping away the tears and ignoring the tantrums.

When analysts equate death with funerary ritual, they assume that rituals encode and store encapsulated wisdom as if it were a microcosm of the informal workings of everyday life in a culture. Johannes Fabian, for example, found during the decade of the 1960s the four major anthropological journals carried only nine papers on death, and most of those "dealt with only with the purely ceremonial aspects of death" (1973:178). The bias that so privileges ritual risks assuming the answers to the questions that most need to be asked. Do rituals, for example, always reveal cultural depth? Huntington and Metcalf simply reflect the received wisdom as they confidently begin their work by affirming that rituals embody "the collective wisdoms of many cultures" (1979:1). Surely this assertion requires investigation.

At the polar extremes, rituals could either display cultural depth or be brimming with platitudes. In the latter instance, rituals could, for example, act as catalysts that precipitate processes whose unfolding occurs over subsequent months or even years.

My own experience fits the platitudes and catalyst model better than the model of microcosmic deep culture. Even a careful analysis of the language and symbolic actions during the two funerals for which I have been a chief mourner could reveal precious little about the lived experience of bereavement.[4] This statement, of course, should not lead anyone to derive universal knowledge from someone else's personal knowledge. Instead, it should encourage ethnographers to ask whether a ritual's wisdom is deep or conventional and whether its process is immediately transformative or but a single step in a lengthy series of ritual and everyday events.

In attempting to grasp the cultural force of rage and other powerful emotional states, one should look both to formal ritual and to the informal emotional states; one should look both to formal ritual and to the informal practices of everyday life. Symbolic analysis, in other words, can be extended from formal ritual to the inclusion of myriad cultural practices less elaborate and circumscribed. Such descriptions can seek out force as well as thickness.

Grief, Rage, and Ilongot Headhunting

Allow me now to sketch how considerations of cultural force apply to Ilongot headhunting. Perhaps we should begin by viewing headhunting as a ritual enactment of expiatory sacrifice. The raid begins with calling the spirit of the potential victim, moves through the ritual of farewell, and continues with seeking favorable omens along the trail. Most Ilongot men speak about hunger and deprivation as they take days to move slowly toward the place where they set up an ambush and await the first person who happens along. Once the raiders kill their victims, they toss away the head rather than keep it as a trophy. Before a raid, men describe their state of being by saying that the burdens of life have made them heavy and entangled, like a tree with vines clinging to it. After a successful raid, they say that they become light of step and ruddy in complexion. The collective energy of the celebration with its song, music, and dance is said to give the participants a sense of well-being. The ritual process involves cleansing and catharsis.

The view just outlined gains analytical power by regarding ritual as a self-contained process. Without denying the insight in this approach, we must also consider its limitations. Suppose, for example, we view exorcism rituals as if they were complete in themselves and never consider them as parts of larger processes unfolding before and after the ritual period. What can we say about the state of being demented through possession? Through what processes does someone recover or continue to be afflicted when rituals fail? Failure to consider these questions can rob the force from the afflictions and therapies only partially actualized during the formal ritual. Still other questions could apply, not only to the person afflicted but also to such differently positioned subjects, as the healer and the audience. In all cases the problem involves the delineation of processes that occur before and after, as well as during, the ritual moment.

If the position just outlined critically can be called the *microcosmic view*, I should like to propose an alternative called *ritual as a busy intersection*. Rather than a self-contained sphere of deep cultural activity, ritual can be seen as a place where a number of distinct social processes intersect. The crossroads simply provide a space for distinct trajectories to traverse rather than containing them in complete encapsulated form. From this perspective, Ilongot headhunting can be seen as standing at the confluence of three analytically separable processes.

The first process concerns whether or not it is an opportune time to raid. In the past, historical conditions determined raiding patterns, ranging along a spectrum from frequent to likely to unlikely to impossible. These conditions, for example, have included American colonial efforts at pacification, the Great Depression, World War II, revolutionary movements in the surrounding lowlands, feuding among Ilongot groups, and the declaration of martial law in 1972. Ilongots themselves speak of such historical contingencies by analogy with hunting. Hunters say that one's opportunities lie beyond one's control, for who can say whether game will cross one's path or whether one's arrow will strike its target. My book on Ilongot headhunting explores these historical factors at some length (R. Rosaldo 1980).

Second, young men coming of age undergo a protracted period

of personal turmoil during which they desire nothing so much as to take a head. It is a time when they seek a life partner and contemplate the traumatic dislocation of leaving their families of origin and entering their new wife's household as a stranger. Young men weep, sing, and burst out in anger because of their intense, fierce desire to take a head and wear the coveted red hornbill earrings that adorn the men who have, as Ilongot say, arrived (*tabi*) before them. Volatile, envious, and passionate, at least according to their own cultural stereotype of the young unmarried man (*buintaw*), they constantly lust to take a head. During the initial period of Ilongot fieldwork, Shelly and I had abandoned our unmarried youths only the year before; hence our ready empathy with late-adolescent turbulence. Her book on Ilongot notions of self explores the passionate anger of young men in considerable depth (M. Rosaldo 1980).

Third, older men are rather differently positioned than their younger counterparts. Because they have already beheaded somebody, they can wear the red hornbill earrings so coveted by youths. Thus their desire to headhunt grows less from chronic adolescent turmoil than from more intermittent acute agonies of loss. After the death of somebody to whom they are closely attached, older men often vow to punish themselves until they participate in a successful headhunting raid. These deaths can cover a range of instances from literal death through natural causes or beheading to social death where, for example, a man's wife runs off with another man. All these cases share the rage born of devastating loss. This anger at abandonment is irreducible in that nothing at a deeper level explains it. Although symbolic analysis often argues against the dreaded last analysis, the linkage of grief, rage, and headhunting has reached rock bottom.

It is evident that my earlier understandings of Ilongot headhunting missed the full significance of how older men experience loss and rage. The position of older men proves critical in this context because they, and not the youths, set the processes of headhunting in motion. Their rage is intermittent, whereas that of youths is continuous. Thus, in the equation of headhunting, older men are the variable and younger men are the constant. Culturally speaking, older men are endowed with knowledge and stamina that their juniors have not yet attained, hence they care for (*saysay*) and lead (*bukur*) the younger men when they raid.

In a preliminary survey of the literature on headhunting, I found that the lifting of mourning prohibitions frequently occurs after taking a head. Compared with reported notions, for example, that men cut off human heads in order to acquire either soul stuff or personal names (see McKinley 1976; Needham 1976; M. Rosaldo 1977), this account of youthful anger and older men's rage born of devastating loss lends greater human plausibility to the notion that headhunters can find their cultural practices compelling. Because the discipline correctly refuses to say that by nature headhunters are bloodthirsty, it must construct convincing explanations of how headhunters create an intense desire to cut off human heads. Hence, the significance in seeking an account of passions that animate human conduct by exploring the cultural force of the emotions.

Emotion, Ritual, and the Positioned Subject

Of the four major assertions made in this essay, the initial two concern problems that emerge from assuming a correct answer instead of raising a question that requires investigation; the latter two outline certain methodological consequences of speaking about the positioned subject.

1. Does cultural depth always equal cultural elaboration? Think of the speaker who is filibustering. The language used can sound elaborate as it heaps word upon word, but surely it is not deep. Depth, in other words, should be separated from the presence or absence of elaboration. By the same token, one-liners can be vacuous or pithy.

The concept of force calls attention to an enduring intensity in human conduct, which can occur with or without the dense elaboration conventionally associated with cultural depth. Although relatively without elaboration in speech, song, or ritual, the rage of older Ilongot men who have suffered devastating losses proves enormously consequential in that, foremost among other things, it leads them to behead their fellow humans. Thus, the notion of force involves both affective intensity and significant consequences that unfold over a long period of time.

2. Do rituals always encapsulate deep cultural wisdom? Could they instead contain the wisdom of Polonius? Certain rituals, of course, both reflect and create ultimate values, key cultural conceptions, and the bases of group solidarity. In other cases, however, they bring people together and deliver a set of platitudes that enable them to go on with their lives rather than offer them insight.

Rituals can thus serve as the vehicles for processes that occur both before and after the period of their performance. Funeral rituals, for example, do not contain all the processes of mourning. It is a mistake to collapse the two because neither ritual nor mourning fully encapsulates or fully explains the other. In such cases the ritual process can be only a resting point along a number of longer processual trajectories; hence, the image of ritual as a crossroads where distinct life processes can intersect.

3. The ethnographer, as a positioned subject, can grasp certain ethnographic phenomena better than others. Most simply, the concept of position refers to a structural location from which one has a particular angle of vision. Consider, for example, how age, gender, being an outsider, and association with a neocolonial regime can influence what one learns.

Position can also refer to how one's lived experience both enables and inhibits particular kinds of insight. Nothing in my own experience, for example, had equipped me even to imagine the anger possible in bereavement. It was not until after Shelly's death in 1981 that I was in a position to grasp the force of what Ilongots had repeatedly told me about grief, rage, and headhunting.

4. Natives, as positioned subjects, also have their insights and blindness. This essay considers both the structural positions of older versus younger men and how lived experience positions chief mourners differently from those less involved. In reviewing anthropological writings on death, I often simply shifted the

analysis from the position of those least involved to that of the chief mourners.

From this perspective the positions of the ethnographer and the native should be considered in conjunction with one another. The following remarks by Pierre Bourdieu, despite his unforgivable use of the masculine pronoun, seem apposite here:

> The anthropologist's particular relation to the object of his study contains the makings of a theoretical distortion inasmuch as his situation as an observer, excluded from the real play of social activities by the fact that he has no place (except by choice or by way of a game) in the system observed and has no need to make a place for himself there, inclines him to a hermeneutic representation of practices, leading him to reduce all social situations to communicative relations and, more precisely, to decoding operations. . . . And exaltation of the virtues of the distance secured by externality simply transmutes into an epistemological choice the anthropologist's objective situation, that of the "impartial spectator," as Husserl puts it, condemned to see all practice as spectacle. (Bourdieu 1977:1)

Similarly, most anthropologists write about death as if they were positioned as uninvolved spectators who have no lived experience that could provide knowledge about the cultural force of emotions.

Notes

Field research among the Ilongots, conducted over thirty months during 1967–69 and 1974, was financed by a National Science Foundation predoctoral fellowship, by National Science Foundation Research Grants GS-1509 and GS-40788, and a Mellon Award for junior faculty from Stanford University. A Fulbright Grant financed a two-month stay in the Philippines during 1981. This essay has benefitted from the comments of Jane Atkinson, Edward Bruner, Roberto DaMatta, Louise Lamphere, Rick Maddox, Kirin Narayan, Emiko Ohnuki-Tierney, Mary Pratt, Amelie Rorty, and Maidi Rosenblatt.

This essay is reprinted from *Text, Play, and Story: 1983 Proceedings of the American Ethnological Society* edited by Edward Bruner. Washington, D.C., 1984, pp. 178–95.

1. Force and related concepts, particularly those concerning emotions, have long been part of the anthropological vocabulary (see, e.g., H. Geertz 1959). In *Islam Observed* (1968), Clifford Geertz found it necessary to distinguish the force of cultural patterning from its scope as he delineated the contrasts between Moroccan and Javanese forms of mysticism. He states the distinction between force and scope in this manner: "By 'force' I mean the thoroughness with which such a pattern is internalized in the personalities of the individuals who adopt it, its centrality or marginality in their lives. . . . By 'scope,' on the other hand, I mean the range of social contexts within which religious considerations are regarded as having more or less direct relevance" (1968:111–12).

In his later works, Geertz develops the notion of scope more than that of force. My use of the term *force* differs from that of Geertz in stressing the concept of the positioned subject rather than processes of internalization within individual personalities.

2. Lest the hypothesis Insan rejected appears utterly implausible, I should mention that among the Berawan of Borneo "death has a chain reaction quality to it. There is a considerable anxiety that, unless something is done to break the chain, death will follow upon death. The logic of this is now plain: The unquiet soul kills, and so creates more unquiet souls" (Metcalf 1982:127). The Berawan, in other words, link a version of exchange theory to headhunting.

3. Like Douglas, Huntington and Metcalf conflate death and mortuary ritual by announcing the former in their title and specifying the latter in their subtitle.

4. Arguably, ritual works differently for those most affected versus those least affected by a particular death. Funerals may distance the former from overwhelming emotional states, whereas they may draw the latter closer to strongly felt sentiments (see Scheff 1979). Such matters can be investigated through the notion of the positioned subject.

Works Cited

Bourdieu Pierre. 1977. *Outline of a Theory of Practice.* Cambridge: Cambridge University Press.

de Beauvoir, Simone. 1969. *A Very Easy Death.* Harmondsworth, UK: Penguin.

Douglas, William A. 1969. *Death in Murelaga: Funerary Ritual in a Spanish Basque Village*. Seattle: University of Washington Press.

Fabian, Johannes. 1973. "How Others Die—Reflections on the Anthropology of Death." In *Death in American Experience*, edited by A. Mack, 177–201. New York: Schocken.

Geertz, Clifford. 1968. *Islam Observed*. New Haven: Yale University Press.

————. 1974. *The Interpretation of Cultures*. New York: Basic Books.

Geertz, Hildred. 1959. "The Vocabulary of Emotion: A Study of Javanese Socialization Processes." *Psychiatry* 22:225–37.

Huntington, Richard, and Peter Metcalf. 1979. *Celebrations of Death: The Anthropology of Mortuary Ritual*. Cambridge: Cambridge University Press.

McKinley, Robert. 1976. "Human and Proud of It! A Structural Treatment of Headhunting Rites and the Social Definition of Enemies." In *Studies in Borneo Societies:Social Process and Anthropological Explanation*, edited by G. Appell, 92–126. DeKalb, IL: Center for Southeast Asian Studies, Northern Illinois University.

Metcalf, Peter. 1982. *A Borneo Journey into Death: Berawan Eschatology from Its Rituals*. Philadelphia: University of Pennsylvania Press.

Needham, Rodney. 1976. "Skulls and Casuality." *Man* 11:71–88.

Rosaldo, Michelle. 1977. "Skulls and Casuality." *Man* 12:168–70.

————. 1980. *Knowledge and Passion: Ilongot Notions of Self and Social Life*. Cambridge: Cambridge University Press.

Rosaldo, Renato. 1980. *Ilongot Headhunting, 1883–1973: A Study in Society and History*. Stanford: Stanford University Press.

Scheff, T. J. 1979. *Catharsis in Healing, Ritual, and Drama*. Berkeley: University of California Press.

Wilson, Godfrey. 1939. *Nyakyusa Conventions of Burial*. Johannesburg: The University of the Witwatersrand Press.

INDEX

*

cultural wisdom in, 135; death/
funerary, 126–30, 135, 137n4;
exorcism, 132; headhunting,
131–34; microcosmic view of,
132; vs. mourning, 128, 130,
135; as obligatory behavior, 127,
130; sentiment created by, 127;
weeping/wailing, 127–28
Rosaldo, Michelle Zimbalist: ar-
rival in Mungayang, 110; death
of, 101, 123–24; Ilongot studies
by, 133; in the Philippines,
111–12
Rosaldo, Renato: arrival in Munga-
yang, 110; "Father Joe," 110;
"How Do I, Renato, Know That
Manny Knows," 102–3, 104; on
how the poems were written,
104–5; "In a White Cubicle,"
108; "I Was Walking," 103; loss
of his brother, 123, 124; "The
Omen of Mungayang," 102; in
the Philippines, 111–12; social

relations on the day of Shelly's
death, 107–10; "The Soldier,"
109; "The Tricycle Taxi Driver,"
109–10

Sapir, Edward, 113
science, purification of, 112
scope vs. force, 137n1
Shapiro, Harvey, 106
Singleton, Anne (*pseud. of* Ruth
Benedict), 113
"The Soldier" (R. Rosaldo), 109
"Sunday in the Empty Nest"
(Olds), 106

thick description, 106, 117
"The Tricycle Taxi Driver"
(R. Rosaldo), 109–10
Turner, Victor, 125

Wilson, Godfrey, 128, 129
word-play studies, 125–26